WAIT TILL

I GET YOU

HOME!

To Pastor Jim —
Thanks for joining our
group and adding to
our lively Bible Study.
I hope you enjoy this
book.
Keep fighting
the good
fight for the faith!

WAIT TILL I GET YOU HOME!

E . W . WOOD

Pleasant Word

Pleasant Word (a division of WinePress Publishing, PO Box 428, Enumclaw, WA 98022) functions only as book publisher. As such, the ultimate design, content, editorial accuracy, and views expressed or implied in this work are those of the author.

Scripture references are taken from the King James Version of the Bible.

ISBN 13: 978-1-4141-0849-0
ISBN 10: 1-4141-0849-4
Library of Congress Catalog Card Number: 2006908390

TABLE OF CONTENTS

PROLOGUE

I hope you're not someone who skips the prologue and jumps right into the body of a book, because if you do, you'll miss my saying "Thanks" for taking a chance and spending your money and time on it. If you received this book second hand or as a gift, then the "Thanks" for spending your time still goes.

While I am on the subject of offering up gratitude, I thank God who sent his only Son to take the death penalty for the sins that mankind has committed, to open heaven's doors for all who accept him. I thank him, too, not only for the words he's given me to write this book, but also for all the times he's picked me up when I've fallen.

Next comes my mother, Doris, who has had to put up with me all these years and who has proofread the manuscript—*many times!* I could write a whole book about her and the way she has handled the many undeserved hard times in her life. Thanks, Ma!

Much thanks also to Catherine Galasso-Vigorito, a nationally published inspirational columnist and author of *A New You,* who has taken time from her extremely busy schedule over the years to send me personal notes of encouragement. Without her inspiration and practical help *Home* would have never become a reality.

Lastly I want to thank the members of Trinity Church, and particularly our Bible Study group, who have added so much to my Christian walk. I won't name names because: (A) They'll get embarrassed, (B) I would feel terrible if I left anyone out.

This book includes a series of articles I'd written for the church newsletter and a considerable amount of brand-new material. The first article appeared on October 2002, and it is from that one that the title of this book is derived. Each article was complete in itself, a format I've maintained here. Additionally there are several longer pieces, two plays, an Appendix containing an outline of the Bible, and a bibliography.

Wait Till I Get You Home can be read all at once or a little at a time—the overall goal being to get you to explore God's Word on a daily basis and to grow in a relationship with the Creator of all things. *Scripture is for everyone—not just clergy people or theologians!* So don't take anyone else's word (including mine) about what it says—read it and decide for yourself!

There are many Bible versions written in modern language to help you, some excellently rendered such as *The Revised Standard Version, The New International Bible, The Good News Bible, and the New Living Translation.* Still, I have found the *King James Version* to be the standard, and it is the source of all the Bible passages quoted here. I recommend you get a copy of it with which to compare any other versions you might acquire. In addition, you should get a good concordance, such as *Strong's.*

The Bible itself will teach you things about God for the rest of your life—it's truly a book you can never finish even if you read it cover to cover. I have found familiar passages that I've read a dozen times, suddenly providing brand new insights. (See *The Vegetarians of Eden,* for example.)

My own spiritual journey began long ago on a warm spring morning as a six year old who was singing *All Things Bright and Beautiful* along with his classmates in Sunday School. Looking out the window into a deep blue sky punctuated by soft, white cumulus clouds, this young lad knew at that moment, without a shadow of a doubt, that the song he was singing was absolutely true. The Lord God *really did* make it all, and though it is nearly fifty years later, this memory is still as sharp and clear as if it had occurred *last* Sunday.

I want you to know that I am not a biblical scholar—just a guy in search of answers—so I don't guarantee I've gotten all of them right. This uncertainty used to bother me until I discovered that even the *real experts* across the ages haven't always arrived at a consensus. In fact, the church that Jesus had prayed would always be one has fragmented into more denominations than I can name. Sometimes the biggest impediments to Jesus' message have been those who have called themselves Christians.

Now we come to a difficult part for me, but one that is necessary, because I think a reader is entitled to know something about the author. The old adage "consider the source" is a valid one, especially in a work of religion. With a certain amount of trepidation, I will dive in.

I am by nature a private person, much more comfortable out alone in the woods than on a crowded street. I have supported myself by any number of unremarkable jobs ranging from grounds keeping to factory work to electronics. I have more than the usual share of faults, and I've made a lot more wrong turns than right ones. I may be a Christian, but I've never claimed to be very good at it.

In short, *I'm no angel.* I particularly wasn't during my late teens and twenties when I'd fallen deep into the bottle. But Jesus has always been there for me, the strongest evidence of which has been my deliverance from alcoholism some twenty-seven years ago. (Smoking took a while longer—I've only been free of that vice for twelve years.) *I therefore know first hand* that God still works miracles, perhaps the most miraculous thing of all being that he bestows them freely on people who don't deserve them—people like me, for example.

You may well ask at this point why a contradiction such as myself would write a book such as this. One reason is that there have been many times my life hasn't been so great. Maybe yours isn't right now, either. Perhaps it was from circumstances beyond your control, or maybe you were like me and sometimes helped make it that way. Maybe you've seen a lot more rainy days than sunny ones.

If this is so, I want to assure you of one constant, one thing you can depend upon in a world full of disappointments, letdowns, betrayals, and lost dreams: God loves you, and he's concerned about you enough that he let his own Son die just to prove it. If you decide to accept Christ's atoning sacrifice of himself to accomplish all that we never could and seek God's will in your life above all else, things *will* begin to change. Now I'm not talking of inheriting a million or so from long lost Uncle Joe or having all your problems suddenly vanish. They may even get worse. Some of the most horrendous things are reserved for the best people. Look what happened to God's only Son.

What *does* happen is that you won't have to face adversity all alone any more. Best of all, when God decides it's time for you to end your journey on Earth, you'll have a place to go beyond your greatest dreams and expectations. All the hurt will be gone, and you'll live forever in the presence of God himself and his Son along with untold multitudes of angelic hosts and people who have trusted in the Lord since the dawn of time. Until that happens, though, God has left us the Bible, his "Survival Manual." In this book, I'll share with you some of the things it has shown me, things that continue to give me hope in a world that does its best to crush each of us down underfoot.

Another reason I've written *Home* has been that in the past few years I've felt compelled to get deeper into God's Word and to share it with others, and, quite frankly, to try to get my own act together and live more in line with Jesus' teachings. Like Belshazzar of old, I am very much weighed in the balance and found wanting. I have an ever-increasing *sense of urgency* when I see around us signs that things just can't keep going on the way that they have much longer.

The one common denominator to all these ills, of course, lies in the fact that we have walked farther and farther away from the One who created us and the ways he would have us live and act toward him and toward each other. For those who are fearful of Twenty-First Century earth you have good reason—and plenty of company.

Despite this, I want to show you that there is all the more reason for hope, because there is Someone who will *always* be there for us, and that same Someone will one day make it *all right!* Through the growing darkness which continues to march across our planet, I can still see those soft, white clouds in that sky of depthless blue, and know the Master is still there and showing me the way back home.

Let him come and show you the way, too!

May God's Peace be with you,

E. W. Wood

PART-I

GOD, HIS CREATION, AND YOU

WHERE DO WE FIT IN?

When I consider thy heavens, the work of thy fingers, the moon and the stars, which thou hast ordained; What is man, that thou art mindful of him? and the son of man, that thou visitest him?

—Psalm 8:3-4

CHAPTER ONE

WAIT TILL I GET
YOU HOME!

Ever have your parents lay these fear-inspiring words on you?
Big time trouble! You'd pushed the envelope, crossed the line,
made a BIG MISTAKE! You knew you were going to find out just
how big you messed up once "They Got You Home!"

I was having a nice long walk out in the New England woods
on a crisp autumn day; a soft breeze was blowing gently through
the trees. Several times on my trip, I encountered an area where the
sun brilliantly illuminated the yellow-leaved sugar maples against
the backdrop of the deep blue fall sky. I knew that this was all created by the hand of the Master Artist. The words of St. Paul came
immediately to mind:

> *But as it is written, Eye hath not seen, nor ear heard, neither have
> entered into the heart of man, the things which God hath prepared
> for them that love him.*
>
> —1 Corinthians 2:9

And this passage where Jesus had said:

> *"In my Father's house are many mansions: if it were not so, I would
> have told you. I go to prepare a place for you. And if I go and prepare
> a place for you, I will come again, and receive you unto myself; that
> where I am, ye may be also."*
>
> —John 14:2-3

15

So what's the message we're being told? Paul tells us in his first letter to the church in Corinth that heaven is better than hiking a woodland trail on a sunny New England autumn day. Better even than our wildest dreams or our greatest hopes. Better than…well, *anything* because the Lord himself, in John's Gospel, says that he's making a place right there in his Father's house for all those who believe in him.

Yeah, we've been bad. We deserve to be punished. But with Jesus, we know that by trusting in his mercy, by believing in who he is and what he has done for us, we know we won't be.

I can imagine Jesus speaking those very words, "Wait till I get you home!" But when he says it, it's not scary at all, because when we finally get there after our earthly journey, it's gonna be *great!*

CHAPTER TWO

THE GIFT OF WATER

In the beginning God created the heaven and the earth. And the earth was without form, and void; and darkness was upon the face of the deep. And the Spirit of God moved upon the face of the waters.
—Genesis 1:1-2

So begins the story of the creation. Isn't it interesting that within the first two verses of the incredible library which we call the Bible, we find reference to *water?* In the United States we are blessed with vast quantities of clean potable water, so much so that we scarcely give it a thought, except perhaps when the plumbing goes south, a pipe freezes, or a loss of power shuts down our household pump. Throughout much of the world, however, the search for adequate water supplies is becoming a bigger concern than that of the dwindling of oil reserves. After all, it is possible to live without oil, it is *not* without water.

Composed of two atoms of hydrogen, the simplest, most abundant element in the universe, plus an atom of common oxygen, we get this remarkable compound unexcelled in versatility. Now without getting into the debate of creationism, intelligent design, or pure evolution, I think it is safe to say that God used water as the essential ingredient to bring forth and sustain the abundance of life on this planet.

In the past few decades our machines have probed other worlds and listened to the stars. The Hubble Space Telescope has given us breathtaking views from distant regions of the universe, yet in all that immensity we have yet to conclusively prove that there is anyone or anything out there alive, except us. Even if it does happen one day, don't be surprised to find it swimming around something as tiny as a film of water surrounding a buried grain of sand on Mars or adrift in an immense subsurface ocean of sea water on Europa.

There is much more significance to water than just biology. Consider these events from the Bible:

In Genesis we read of a flood of water sent to destroy and wash away from the earth the race of humans which had become so corrupt and evil that God regretted ever having made them in the first place. Only eight were spared—Noah and his family—the only decent people God could find out of them all. We read of the covenant of the rainbow where God promised he would never use another deluge to destroy all the creatures which walk on dry land (Genesis 6, 7, 8).

The sons of Israel were delivered from their Egyptian overlords through a miraculously parted Red Sea (Exodus 14:21-31).

The Gospels take us back to the time of John and his ministry of baptizing for repentance with the water of the Jordan River. Jesus himself accepts this baptisim to provide the example that we should follow. Significantly this is, I believe, the only time in history there was a simultaneous *physical* manifestation of the Trinity (John 1:29-34).

So the next time you go over to your sink and turn on the tap, watch the rain fall from the heavens, or walk along the beach, stop and take a good look at that remarkable substance that has been part of us and all that we know, right from the beginning of the world.

HOW BIG IS GOD?

The answer, of course, is that God is infinite, beyond any measure we human beings could ever devise. But have you ever considered just how big "infinite" really is? I was thinking about this as I walked under the stars one cold winter night.

Maybe we can begin to get the idea if we start close to home and then work our way out. Take the earth for example. Our planet is just nearly 8000 miles in diameter. A little math tells us it is about 25,000 miles in circumference. That means it would take you 8333 hours to walk around it—some 347 days or almost a year—if we consider 3 miles per hour an average walking speed. (This assumes that you could also swim that fast over the places covered by ocean, too.) Sounds pretty big, doesn't it? But God is bigger than that.

Okay, let's move out a little farther—say, to the Moon. That's just under a quarter of a million miles away. That's some serious distance. Better start walking now, because that's a 9 year hike. Still, God is bigger than that.

How about the sun? At a distance of 93,000,000 miles, that walk will take you over 3500 years. God is bigger than this, too.

Okay, let's take a big jump to the nearest star besides the Sun. That would be Proxima Centauri at a distance of 4.3 light years or about 25 trillion miles. (Light travels 5.87 trillion miles in a year.) It will take you 950 million years to walk there and still, God is bigger than that.

How about our nearest full-sized galaxy? That would be M-31, in Andromeda, which is at a "modest" 2.8 million light years away. That's 16,436,000,000,000,000,000 (16.436 quintillion) miles. That would take you 617 trillion years to walk that far. Yet God is bigger even than this.

The size of the entire universe is believed to be as big as 15 billion light years. That's 88,050,000,000,000,000,000,000 (88.05 sextillion) miles. You could walk across the entire cosmos in 3,3 48,200,000,000,000,000 (3.3482 quintillion) years, and still our infinite God is bigger than even this unimaginable distance.

So the next time you have a problem, take a look up into the night sky, and realize that God is *even bigger than all your troubles!*

BELIEVING IN THE UNSEEN

It might be interesting to consider that for everything you see in the night sky, there's a lot more that you can't. On any given clear, moonless night there are only about 2000 distinct stars visible to the unaided eye. If you throw in the moon, a few planets, and an occasional comet, that's about it. Considering that there are over *100 billion stars* in our galaxy alone and the fact that there are untold billions of galaxies besides ours, you get the idea of how limited our view really is.

But wait…. there's more!

According to current astronomical thought the universe is composed of the following:

1. **Normal matter: 4%.** This includes you, me, the sun, the Earth, and all those stars, planets, comets I've mentioned.
2. **Dark matter: 23%.** This is an exotic form of matter whose influence can be seen in the rate at which a galaxy's component stars revolve. Specifically, the rate of revolution observed is much faster than one would expect from the matter that we can see with our eyes and instruments. In other words, there is a lot more stuff composing the galaxies that we can't detect except by its gravitational effects.

WAIT TILL I GET YOU HOME!

3. **Dark energy: 73%.** Think dark matter is strange? The story becomes stranger still. There is some kind of...*something else*...which appears to be causing the universe to expand faster than expected. Instead of slowing down, the rate at which the galaxies are moving away from each other is increasing. Think about it like this: You're driving your car along a flat roadway and suddenly the engine quits. You quickly shift it into neutral so it will coast as far as it can. Now comes the twist. Instead of slowing down and eventually stopping, the car begins to inexplicably accelerate. (If we could reproduce this effect on a small scale, our energy problems would be a thing of the past, wouldn't they?)

Let's see if we can draw some conclusions from these enigmatic findings.

We know that 96% of all creation will remain invisible to us despite our technology, and it is those unseen components which have the greatest effects on those things which *are* visible. Since this is the case, the fact that God is invisible yet still in control of all that exists does not seem so far-fetched now, does it?

The Psalmist (perhaps King David himself) wrote:

The heavens declare the glory of God; and the firmament sheweth his handywork.
> —Psalm 19:1

St. Paul said:

For the invisible things of him from the creation of the world are clearly seen, being understood by the things that are made.
> —Romans 1:20a

Will we ever know the whole story? *Can* we ever know? The Bible suggests that the answer is a resounding "Yes!" Again, St. Paul tells us:

*For now we see through a glass, darkly; but then face to face: now I
know in part; but then shall I know even as also I am known.*
—1 Cor. 13:12

Here is what Job says:

*For I know that my redeemer liveth, and that he shall stand at the
latter day upon the earth: And though after my skin worms destroy
this body, yet in my flesh shall I see God; Whom I shall see for myself,
and mine eyes shall behold, and not another.*
—Job 19:25-27a

Someday the veil will be lifted, all our questions will be answered, and the Unseen will become Seen when at last we behold
the Artist himself face to face...and not as a stranger!

This is what Jesus did. For you. For me. Forever.

CHAPTER FIVE

THIS THING CALLED TIME

But, beloved, be not ignorant of this one thing, that one day is with the Lord as a thousand years, and a thousand years as one day.
—2 Peter 3:8

We measure it with the ticks of our clocks, the crossing off of the days on our calendars, the passing of the seasons. It passes, second after second, hour after hour, day after day, month after month, year after year, carrying us along like a stream into the future.

For as long as man has looked up into the sky, he has watched the movements of the sun, moon, and stars. In his nomadic times, he used them to determine where and when the herds upon which his survival depended would travel. As agriculture developed, the need to know seasons and times became even more important. The Egyptians watched for the bright star Sirius to appear in the sky, knowing that when it did the Nile would undergo its annual flood, refurbishing their fields for the coming year. For most of human history, our ancestors regarded time as a cyclic and unchangeable characteristic of nature. Seasons came and seasons went. People were born, matured, grew old, and died; all to be replaced by succeeding generations. What was, is, and always would be.

24

That view was to change forever when a man named Abram was called forth from his home in Ur of the Chaldees (located in what would become modern day Iraq) to journey to a faraway land that would eventually become the home of his descendants. For the first time in human history, the way things were was *not* always how they would be.

God told Abram (who would become Abraham) and his wife Sarai (Sarah) that their offspring would become as manifold as the stars in the clear night sky. Even more amazing was that one of the nations that would result from their progeny would be a special one, dear to God; a nation through whom the whole world would be blessed (Genesis 22:16-18). Centuries later, Israel would become that chosen people from which God himself would one day come to live among us: Emmanuel—the Savior and Redeemer of us all.

Many of the prophecies of Scripture have been fulfilled since God spoke to Abraham those thousands of years ago. I believe the rest will soon come to pass, including those of an ominous time ahead of unparalleled tribulation, the shadows of which even now seem to be lengthening over our troubled world.

But the last and best part of God's plan for mankind culminates in a wondrous future in which Jesus leads all believers to take up residence in God's house of many rooms (John 14:2-3) and to an endless time beyond when he will personally dwell on Earth and make all things new. (Rev. 21:1-5)

Yet it seems like such a long time since Jesus walked the earth, and still, here we are. Why has Jesus waited so long to return? St. Peter addresses that very question:

> *The Lord is not slack concerning his promise, as some men count slackness; but is longsuffering to us-ward, not willing that any should perish, but that all should come to repentance.*
> —2 Peter 3:9

You see, Jesus is giving humanity plenty of time to make the choice to live with him forever, but no one should take his patience for granted, because Peter also teaches that there will come a day when it will run out—and quite unexpectedly:

But the day of the Lord will come as a thief in the night...
—2 Peter 3:10a

When this happens there will be no more warnings, no more extensions, no more chances. There is much wisdom in what St. Paul says:

For he (God) saith, "I have heard thee in a time accepted, and in the day of salvation have I succoured thee: behold, now is the accepted time; behold, now is the day of salvation."
—2 Cor. 6:2

It sounds to me like *today* is the best one for us to decide where we will spend eternity—*while there is still time!*

CHAPTER SIX

TRANSIT OF VENUS

Back in June 2004, an astronomical event which hasn't happened in over 120 years momentarily gave us a welcome break from the usual strife and conflict which generally comprises the daily news. Venus passed between the sun and the Earth. I was fortunate enough to have a clear view of this event, seeing it first hand through my small telescope. Sure enough, there it was—a small circle backlit by the sun. I watched as the tiny black disk slowly crept toward the sun's edge, touching it, then appearing as a notch before leaving completely. Though I have often seen Venus as a brilliant morning or evening star, this view was certainly unique.

As I watched, I considered that I was looking upon an entire world, almost equal in size to our own planet, in silhouette against the backdrop of the same sun that lights our own blue skies. Of course, with its deadly shroud of sulfuric acid clouds, dense carbon dioxide atmosphere, and 800+ degree F. surface temperature, the resemblance between that hellish world and our own cool, ocean-covered Earth ends, save for its gravitational pull. (In other words, you'd weigh about the same on Venus as you do down here, provided you were ever tempted to try landing there.)

As a matter of fact, if you take a gander around our solar system, it seems a lot easier to make awful planets than pleasant ones, at least as far as building suitable homes for sentient beings goes. This may be true universally. In all the SETI searches of deep space, so far we have no evidence of any other self-aware beings anyplace else than Earth. This strikes me as strange in a cosmos that statistically should be swarming with life and artificially produced radio traffic.

What if *it is only us?*

Nowhere in the Bible, to my knowledge, are we told of sentient life on other worlds. Nor is it mentioned that human beings will ever permanently live off the Earth in this present age. Now it isn't as if the Bible shied away from topics of extraordinary events: Ezekiel's wheels, Elijah's departure, and visions of heaven from Daniel, St. Paul, St. John, and a multitude of others. We are even told of intelligent beings (e.g. angels, etc.) in heaven, but none in our own realm. For me it suggests these questions:

1. Did God do all of creation—*just for us?*
2. If this is so, what does it tell us of his love for us, even giving his own Son to die for our benefit as well?
3. How should we therefore act toward God in the face of his overwhelming generosity?

I know myself that when I consider these points, I see the need to improve, though not for salvation's sake. Jesus has already accomplished that for me at the cross.

It's really more of a matter of saying "Thank you" to the One who did it all for me.

WHAT IS MAN...?

When I consider thy heavens, the work of thy fingers, the moon and the stars which thou has ordained: What is man, that thou art mindful of him?

—Psalm 8:3-4

On a summer day almost forty years ago, these words were spoken by Buzz Aldrin from a fragile metal spaceship returning from the blackness of space thousands of miles away. Astronauts Armstrong and Aldrin were the first human beings ever to see the sight of the cloud-sheathed blue place we call Earth from the surface of the battered, lifeless, monochromatic world over which Mike Collins orbited alone in their tiny ship.

As I write, a couple of intrepid robotic explorers still roll across the arid Martian landscape, over 35 million miles away, sending back images of a cold, desert world of peach colored skies and blue clouds. A probe called "Huygens" has since streaked into the thick orange atmosphere of Titan, Saturn's huge moon, showing us an incredibly distant, frigid world of methane rivers and lakes. The New Horizon ship is now on its way, traveling at over 30,000 miles per hour, to Pluto, that strange mini-world, whose journey carries it alternately closer to the sun than Neptune and then almost twice that distance on its centuries-long orbit. Yet as intriguing as these far-off places are, Earth remains a living marvel floating in the black sea of space. Again the question comes forth: *What is man?*

So queried the psalmist as he looked upon the moon and stars with the same awe with which mankind has pondered the nocturnal sky ever since Adam and Eve first drew breath. In the immensity of the star-strewn night I myself often wonder, *Why, Lord, do you think about us at all?*

What is man, so flawed, so small in the scheme of God's creation, that he merits the Master's special attention? What does the Creator see in us that caused him to send his own Son into our world to give his own life to fix what we had so terribly broken? Out of all the universe, out of all living creatures, why have we been endowed with the capacity to look up and ask these questions; to have the ability to seek out the One who is the Father of us all? As our instruments reach across the vastness of the cosmos, we have yet to see any indication that anyone or anything else ever has.

What is man that God chose to build our world and us out of elements forged in the stars, cast out across the universe untold ages ago? Did you realize that the dust of which the Bible tells us we are formed (Gen 2:7) is actually *stardust?*

What is man that, through Jesus, is promised an everlasting future with the Author of all that was, is, and ever will be? This is the mystery that will forever elude us until that day when we at last behold God's face and learn the answer from the Maker himself—when we walk with him for eternity beyond the heavens.

CHAPTER EIGHT

WHY INTELLIGENCE?

So God created man in his own image, in the image of God created he him; male and female created he them.
—Genesis 1:27

Whether you take the story of the creation from the Bible literally or from the standpoint of intelligent design, which attempts to meld God and science, we find that the last of God's creation is…us! By the way, before you ask, I left out the third premise of our orderly cosmos being the product of totally random events. To me that's akin to throwing a bunch of gears and parts in a bag, giving it a good shake, and ending up with a perfectly operating alarm clock when you get done. This just seems too outlandish for me. But now, let's go on.

I'm sure that the world would continue to function very well without self-aware, conscious entities, such as ourselves, living on it. The rains would fall, winds would blow, seasons would pass, plants and animals would get along just fine (probably a lot better, sometimes) *without* us. Earth would still be an Eden.

But…*here we are!* And that begs the question: Why?

Perhaps the first chapter of Genesis gives us a clue. We are told that God turned the world and everything in it over to the first two humans to enjoy and share with him. Amazingly, even when Adam and Eve betrayed his trust, he did not abandon them or their offspring. Indeed, he "stayed in touch" throughout the entirety of our history, seeking to restore us back to the relationship we once had with him in the dim beginnings of time. To be sure, this has not reached its culmination, which is painfully evident in a world which spins farther and farther away from the original plan God had for us.

Yet even in the face of our continued defiance as a race, we are assured that one day we *will* be brought back into his presence—we have his guarantee in his Word.

Still I wonder...*why?*

Perhaps it has something to do with what St. Paul told the elders of the church of Ephesus:

> *"Remember the words of the Lord Jesus, how he said, 'It is more blessed to give than to receive.'"*
>
> —Acts 20:35b

Don't we have before us the greatest example of *giving* in the fact that God himself gave us our world, our reason, and, most of all, *even his own Son?*

On second thought, maybe we'd better offer up some "Thank you's" to go along with all those "Why's."

CHAPTER NINE

INTO THE LIGHT

In the beginning was the Word, and the Word was with God, and the Word was God. The same was in the beginning with God. All things were made by him; and without him was not any thing made that was made. In him was life; and the life was the light of men. And the light shineth in darkness; and the darkness comprehended it not. There was a man sent from God, whose name was John. The same came for a witness, to bear witness of the Light, that all men through him might believe. He was not that Light, but was sent to bear witness of that Light. That was the true Light, which lighteth every man that cometh into the world.

—John 1:1-9

The lengthening of the days of spring is always remarkable to me after a long, cold winter. There is a reassuring increase of the strength of the sun's rays as it climbs ever higher in the sky, and there is at last the sense that soon an explosion of color will replace the whites and grays of our monochromatic New England winter. Even more significant is how the returning light lifts our very moods.

In the verses above, John tells us that our entire universe exists because of Jesus—all the matter and energy comprising *everything.* Jesus is *light,* John tells us above. I have personally come across thirty passages concerning *light* and its connection with God or Jesus in the Bible and there are many more.

Even in the world of science *light* holds enormous importance. One hundred years ago, Albert Einstein discovered just how fundamental it is to the mechanics of the cosmos. We've learned:

1. Energy and matter are actually different forms of the same thing, their relationship actually defined by light's velocity. ($E = mc2$)
2. Light always travels 186,000 miles per second in a vacuum.
3. Light is capable of transversing the vastness of space. The Hubble Space Telescope can see objects many billions of light years away by the light they emit.
4. There is a background microwave radiation present throughout the universe. (Microwaves are a form of electromagnetic radiation, just like light, but of a lower frequency than can be seen directly by human vision. They are easily detectable by a proper antenna just like a radio signal. Your microwave oven generates them to warm up your dinner and all those cell phones use them to operate as well—making them a mixed blessing, perhaps?)

Now, just as a painting reveals something of the artist that created it, or a book part of its author's personality, is it any surprise that the cosmos reveals in the universality of light the fact that its Creator is the Father of Lights? (James 1:17)

Paul said: *For the invisible things of him from the creation of the world are clearly seen, being understood by the things that are made, even his eternal power and Godhead; so that they are without excuse* (Romans 1:20).

Isn't it fascinating that the more we learn about nature, the more we see the truth of this passage? Isn't it even more intriguing that the Bible beat the scientists by a few thousand years?

THE OUTSIDER

He came unto his own, and his own received him not. But as many as received him, to them gave he power to become the sons of God, even to them that believe on his name.

—John 1:11-12

Do you go through the motions of living in the world but finding that there is just something undefinable keeping you from feeling completely at home or from totally fitting in? I'm sure most people have from time to time. Now I'm not talking about such a profound detachment, indicating some serious physical or psychological problem. It is more like a sense that nothing the world has to offer ever completely fills the cup.

Let me tell you a story of a man who lived very far away.

Two thousand years ago, in Judea, a tiny baby was born to a carpenter and his wife. Even before his birth, they knew the child they were to have and raise was like no other. Over the course of the next thirty years, he grew into manhood and was apparently well-liked.

And Jesus increased in wisdom and stature, and in favour with God and man.

—Luke 2:52

And then something began to change.

After his baptism and testing in the desert, this young man suddenly began to make strange statements about the existence of another kingdom, one in which those who were last in this world would become first in the new one (Matthew 19:30) and where wealth as it was measured by human standards was of no value at all (Matthew 19:21-29).

He had collected about himself a curious, varied group including fishermen, a tax collector, and even a revolutionary (Matthew 10:2-4). For three years this unusual company traveled together. At first, Jesus and his friends were warmly received, but as time passed, there was a growing opposition to this wandering rabbi and his followers. Even his own neighbors didn't accept him for who he was (Matthew 13:54-58). This sentiment grew more widespread as Jesus' ministry spread, especially among the religious leaders of those days that he confounded with his wisdom.

I often reflect upon the dispair he must have felt as he looked upon Jerusalem, lamenting on its stubborn refusal to accept the messages of those whom God had sent to it over the centuries (Matthew 23:37), knowing his own death was soon to come (Matthew 16:21). It would be made all the more bitter in that the betrayal, for just a few pieces of silver, would be at the hands of one of those he had loved and taught (Matthew 27:3-5), while the rest of his closest friends fled into that terrible night when the authorities came to arrest him (Matthew 26:56).

But it was to get worse—*much, much worse.*

"*My God, my God,*" Jesus called out in anguish as he hung dying a slow death on that hard wooden cross, "*Why hast thou forsaken me?*" (Matthew 27:46b), echoing the lament of Psalm 22:1 written many centuries earlier. Though many scholars have debated the significance of these words over the ages, one thing seems clear—for one terrible moment in time, Jesus found himself totally alone as he paid the price for the transgressions of us all to God, who in his holiness and perfection, can't even *look* upon sin (Habbakkuk 1:13).

Yet this was not the end but a beginning, wherein we can become God's adopted sons and daughters. Jesus has opened this new life for all who believe in his name. One day you and I will go to that place where, for the first time ever, we will truly be at home, welcomed by the Master himself as members of his own family.

And we won't ever be outsiders any more.

CHAPTER ELEVEN

CHRISTIANS AND JEWS

For I (Paul) could wish that myself were accursed from Christ for my brethren, my kinsmen according to the flesh: Who are Israelites; to whom pertaineth the adoption, and the glory, and the covenants, and the giving of the law, and the service of God, and the promises; Whose are the fathers, and of whom as concerning the flesh Christ came, who is over all, God blessed for ever. Amen.
—Romans 9:3-5

If you read and believe the Bible, it is the tale of mankind's fall in Eden and God's long and hard task to try to bring us back to himself—a goal that Scripture says will one day be achieved. God chose the Jews to be the instruments through which he worked to convey his message of salvation, culminating in Jesus Christ the Son, not only of God but also of a young Jewish woman named Mary.

Therefore, to be antisemitic is to deny the truth of both the Hebrew Bible and the Christian New Testament, which the above passage from Romans makes clear. To my mind, therefore, no one who professes to *be* a Christian can hate the people that brought us God's messages and among whom Jesus was born, grew up, and preached. It furthermore denies the race of the first apostles. It disregards Jesus' own wishes to "forgive them, for they know

38

not what they do," and history is replete with horrific examples of people who chose to do just that. Today, this still continues with increasing vehemence.

The fact that the Jews have survived to this day, despite all persecutions, strikes me as nothing less than miraculous. They have now reclaimed their ancestral lands, making them fertile once again, even though they are surrounded by enemies who have tried more than once to exterminate them. The Hebrew language, once as dead as Latin, has come back to life. The ancient Sandhedrin, once the Jewish Supreme Court on both religious and secular matters, was reborn in 2004.

It appears to me that all these incredible events are possible only through acts of divine intervention—a reality which I feel no professing Christian can ignore. Lest we forget, it was a very Jewish Jesus who came to save us from the sinful nature that we had all inherited from Adam and Eve's act of disobedience in Eden—the consequences of which have all too often colored the history of humankind with cruelty and blood.

For too long persecution of the Jews was conveniently justified by the premise that Christ died at their hands. I think the truth is something much more sobering and a lot closer at hand than one might think.

Where do I look to see who really crucified Jesus Christ?

Only into the nearest mirror.

PART-II

HOPE IN A HOPELESS WORLD

FINDING SOME LIGHT IN A DARK PLACE

(Jesus said) "In the world ye shall have tribulation: but be of good cheer; I have overcome the world."

—John 16:33b

CHAPTER ONE

WARS AND RUMORS OF WAR

(Jesus told his disciples) "And ye shall hear of wars and rumours of wars: see that ye be not troubled: for all these things must come to pass, but the end is not yet."

—Matthew 24:6

In less than two months the military campaign in Iraq was over, surprising even the experts in it's rapidity and deft execution. Thankfully, the dire threats of potential chemical, biological, and nuclear attacks on our troops never materialized. But little did we know what was to follow as we tried to rebuild a country ravaged by tyranny and war, against the backdrop of senseless acts of violence from some of the very people we were attempting to help.

I am sure Jesus saw this war from the beginning of time, along with all of the others that have been and will be fought. I am equally sure that this knowledge brought him no comfort, knowing human history would be so tragic—the path our original ancestors chose for us in the dim past.

Still the Lord tells us not to be alarmed at these conflicts! What a strange thing to say, because there are few events which strike as much horror into the hearts of people than warfare. How can we *not* be alarmed, especially with the unimaginable devastation that modern weapons of battle can inflict? And if that wasn't frightening enough, Matthew 24 tells us that things will be getting a lot worse before they get better! If that's all there was to the story, then we'd be crazy *not* to be alarmed.

But despite the mess we've made of our history, Jesus stepped into the midst of human existence to fix what we had broken. It was so important to him, it cost him his very life. Let's see what else the Bible says about all of this:

Looking at the very last verse in Matthew we find Jesus saying to his disciples, *"Lo, I am with you alway, even unto the end of the world. Amen"* (Matthew 28:20b).

In John 16:33b, Jesus also says, *"In the world ye shall have tribulation: but be of good cheer; I have overcome the world."*

In John 14:1-3 he again says, *"Let not your heart be troubled: ye believe in God, believe also in me. In my Father's house are many mansions: if it were not so, I would have told you. I go to prepare a place for you. And if I go and prepare a place for you, I will come again, and receive you unto myself; that where I am, there ye may be also."*

St. Paul also reassures us with these comforting words:

Behold, I shew you a mystery; We shall not all sleep, but we shall all be changed, In a moment, in the twinkling of an eye, at the last trump: for the trumpet shall sound, and the dead shall be raised incorruptible, and we shall be changed. For this corruptible must put on incorruption, and this mortal must put on immortality. So when this corruptible shall have put on incorruption, and this mortal shall have put on immortality, then shall be brought to pass the saying that is written, Death is swallowed up in victory.
—1 Corinthinans 15:51-54

For which cause we faint not; but though our outward man perish, yet the inward man is renewed day by day. For our light affliction, which is but for a moment, worketh for us a far more exceeding and eternal weight of glory.
—2 Corinthinans 4:16-17

For God hath not appointed us to wrath, but to obtain salvation by our Lord Jesus Christ.
—1 Thessalonians 5:9

Believe it or not, these are just a few examples of the hopeful words for all who believe in Jesus. None of us are promised that life in this world will be without troubles and concerns—quite the opposite. Yes, for the immediate future, things will definitely get worse. But through it all, Jesus will be there with you now and forever.

It's guaranteed in God's Word—and that's good enough for me.

CHAPTER TWO

THE GOD OF GOOD SURPRISES

But as it is written, Eye hath not seen, nor ear heard, neither have entered into the heart of man, the things which God hath prepared for them that love him.

—1 Corinthinans 2:9

Over four thousand years ago, an old couple who believed they would die childless were told that not only would they have children but also that through their descendants all the world would be blessed. This was God's promise to Abraham and Sarah.

Joseph, Abraham's great grandson, sold into slavery by his jealous brothers and given up for dead, rose to prominence in Egypt and ended up saving his father's household from famine. Because of this, his father Jacob and his brothers, of whom all the nation of Israel is descended, would survive.

Moses, a foundling who became a member of the household of the ruler of Egypt, discovered his true lineage to be that of Jacob, the same as those whom the pharaoh had enslaved. After killing an Egyptian who had been mistreating a fellow Hebrew, he fled into the desert of Midian, only to return decades later to free his people from their bondage.

David, a young shepherd, defeated Goliath the giant to free the Israelites from their Philistine masters centuries later.

A young Jewish couple, two thousand years ago, was chosen to bring into the world God's only begotten son, Jesus. In his short tenure on earth, he had brought a new covenant to the world, bestowing miraculous works on the sick, the hurting, and the hopeless; forgiving even those who eventually betrayed him to be crucified by foreign occupiers in the bleakest, darkest moment in human history.

Instead of the story of Jesus coming to a tragic end, God brought him back to life, triumphing over the devil and death, beginning the fulfillment of that long-ago promise to Abraham and Sarah.

We would do well to remember that this same God who has intervened so profoundly at critical moments in history is more than capable of stepping into our own lives and situations this very day. The Creator of our incredible universe is but a prayer away, and he wants to be our friend.

Talk about a surprise!

CHAPTER THREE

BAD NEWS, GOOD NEWS

(Jesus said) "In the world ye shall have tribulation: but be of good cheer; I have overcome the world."

—John 16:33b

I have good news and bad news. Which do you want to hear first? I usually pick the bad news, just to be done with it. Besides, maybe the good news will help counteract it. Jesus' statement above certainly is an example of both types of tidings.

First, we're told right up front that life down here isn't going to be a picnic, a walk in the park, fair, just, or right. Ever notice that good people seem to be on the receiving end of grief a lot more often than bad people? Did you ever wonder why? You aren't alone if you did. Habakkuk, the prophet, was asking the same questions around 650 B.C.(Habakkuk 1:13). It looks like things really haven't changed much on old planet Earth over the past two and a half millennia. Bad things have been happening for a long time, and really bad things have happened to really good people throughout history.

Just look at what happened to Jesus who *never sinned!* Look at what happened to his apostles. Only John died of natural causes.

It is almost as if being a decent person generates some kind of global positioning lock on which the bad things can target. As if that wasn't enough, it is going to get worse. Read Matthew 24. Read the twenty-one judgments of Revelation (chapters 6-16).

But take heart, because it is now time for the good news.

Jesus concludes his statement by saying that he has overcome the world. When he died and was resurrected, he won for all of us who believe in him a victory which will be eternal. Read Revelation chapters 21-22 to learn of God's wondrous future for all those who have accepted his Son. We can live forever some day in that magnificent city of New Jerusalem. No more injustice, pain, sorrow, loneliness. God himself will come to live with us forever, and it will literally be heaven on earth. Have you ever experienced a really great time that you wished would never end? Well, the future God has in mind for you is infinitely better—forever!

As far as getting through the present, Jesus tells us, *"Lo, I am with you alway, even unto the end of the world"* (Matt. 28:20b).

He knows that life here will be difficult; the devil and his followers are desperate and will do anything they can to destroy God's people. They know that soon their number will be up (Rev. 12:12). That's why Jesus is in there with us for the long haul, because by trusting in him, we can be victors over the devil's deceptions. He's busy right now getting our rooms ready in his Father's house (John 14:1-6). Despite all of our faults, God will one day welcome us home with open arms, just like the prodigal son was welcomed by his father (Luke 15:11-24). We already have addresses in God's Kingdom and moving day is coming!

(Jesus said) "Surely I come quickly!" Amen! Even so, come Lord Jesus!

—Revelation 22:20

And that certainly is some good news, isn't it?

CHANGES, CHANGES!

Fall is a season of change. The leaves change color, the days get shorter and chillier. All too soon the warm days of summer fade into the past. I don't know about you, but I have to tell you that most of the time I'm not crazy about change! There is a certain comfort with the familiar. I really think the good old days really were *good old days!* To wit:

1. Cars with 4-speeds, V-8's, dual exhausts, and tail fins were cool.
2. Doo-Wop music was great.
3. Nothing beat an ice cream soda from a real soda fountain.
4. The United States still believed "In God We Trust."
5. God was still welcome on school grounds.
6. A nativity scene on the town green at Christmas wasn't cause for lawsuits.
7. Christmas lights above Main Street were an annual treat.
8. The church still thought the Bible was right.

And…well, you get the idea.

Things sure have changed, haven't they? Between you and me, I'm not very impressed in all the ways that the world which greets us every morning has become increasingly more ominous.

What we really need here is a change for the better, because we just can't keep going on the way we have. Something has to give—and soon! Do you feel it, too? Is there a "still small voice" speaking to you at some level beyond words saying that we are headed on the course toward something dark and terrifying? Believe me, you are *not* alone.

But there is someone you can trust to bring you through it all.

Listen to what the prophet, Joel, who lived around 770 B.C. said:

> *And it shall come to pass afterward, that I will pour out my spirit upon all flesh; and your sons and your daughters shall prophesy, your old men shall dream dreams, your young men shall see visions: And also upon the servants and upon the handmaids in those days will I pour out my spirit.*
>
> —Joel 2:28-29

The Day of Pentecost marked the beginning of this prophecy when the Holy Spirit descended on the apostles as tongues of fire (Acts 2:1-21). That same Spirit is still available to you and me today. Of course we have to say "Yes" to Jesus to receive him. One day there will come a time when nothing *"shall not hurt nor destroy in all my holy mountain: for the earth shall be full of the knowledge of the LORD, as the waters cover the sea"* (Isaiah 11:9).

Until then, what shall we do?

How about reading God's Book?

I find the more I do, the greater a depth it takes on and the more it changes the way I look at the world. It has provided a broader perspective on world events, showing me that these turbulent times are but a precursor of the age to come when God's will *"will be done on earth, as it is in heaven."* Scripture has given everyone who believes the comfort of knowing that God's own Son will be there to carry us through *"even unto the end of the world"* (Matt. 28:20b).

Jesus knew things had to change to restore us to his Father, and he knew it would cost him his very life, but he did it anyway.

I'm looking forward to that day when he comes back—and things finally change for the better!

FOR THE BIRDS!

(Jesus told his disciples) "Therefore I say unto you, Take no thought for your life, what ye shall eat; neither for the body, what ye shall put on. The life is more than meat, and the body is more than raiment. Consider the ravens: for they neither sow nor reap; which neither have storehouse nor barn; and God feedeth them: how much more are ye better than the fowls?...

And seek not ye what ye shall eat, or what ye shall drink, neither be ye of doubtful mind. For all these things do the nations of the world seek after: and your Father knoweth that ye have need of these things. But rather seek ye the kingdom of God; and all these things shall be added unto you. Fear not, little flock; for it is your Father's good pleasure to give you the kingdom."

—Luke 12:22-24,29-32

As I write on this cold winter day, I hear the rustle and the calls of the birds drawn to my feeder. This particular one has a transmitter built into it, piping the sounds of their busy lives right into my kitchen. I know they could do just fine without me—they were here long before us, and God would take care of them the same way he has since they first took flight untold millennia ago. But I'm not so sure I would do well at all without their constant company. They've always been a source of pleasure and fascination to me.

I suppose that first and foremost, my captivation with them is that they can fly—an enviable talent requiring thousands of years of technology and experimentation for us poor, landbound humans to finally achieve. Imagine being free to sail the winds and travel over the landscape at will, without the machinery—wouldn't that be great?

Appealing, too, are their antics, especially those of the blue jays squabbling over the seeds I've set out. Now I know a lot of people don't like these guys, because they're noisy and sometimes raid other birds' nests, but if we consider that people can also be noisy and are not above having eggs for breakfast, it leaves us little room for judgment. Jays also have an affinity for whole peanuts, alerting me with their persistent calls if I am just a little late putting some out for them in the morning. Once so provided, I have seen these colorful birds take the time to select a particular one over another for weight, shape, or both. *They're really smart!*

I think God has greatly enjoyed these particular members of his creation, so much so that he made birds a part of significant events: searchers for dry land after the Flood (Genesis 8:6-12); providers of food for Elijah the prophet (1 Kings 17:1-6); and even in the appearance of the Holy Spirit, as a dove, after Jesus was baptized by his cousin John (Matthew 3:16).

Wouldn't our time be much better spent appreciating these feathered miracles rather than wasting it in the mad dash to surround ourselves with all the things society tells us we must have to be successful and content? Didn't Jesus himself tell us to learn a basic life lesson from them in the Luke passage above?

Now to be honest with you, I am just as guilty of forgetting the Lord's admonition as anyone, but I do find as I grow older that a lot of the things I fussed about in the past really *weren't* worth all the trouble. Maybe it's because I've used up more days in my life than I have left that I've finally begun to see that my time is better spent seeking the things that'll last forever

(Jesus said) "But lay up for yourselves treasures in heaven, where neither moth nor rust doth corrupt, and where thieves do not break through nor steal."

—Matthew 6:20

Some day I'll be there in that place.

And it wouldn't surprise me one bit if my feathered friends show up there, too.

A SPECIAL BIRTHDAY

And when the day of Pentecost was fully come, they were all with one accord in one place. And suddenly there came a sound from heaven as of a rushing mighty wind, and it filled all the house where they were sitting. And there appeared unto them cloven tongues like as of fire, and it sat upon each of them. And they were all filled with the Holy Ghost, and began to speak with other tongues, as the Spirit gave them utterance.

—Acts 2:1-4

It was fifty days after Jesus had been resurrected and only ten days since the apostles saw him ascend to heaven in a cloud. The angelic messengers promised that he would one day return in like manner (Acts 1:9-11). Now Jesus' promise to send the Counselor, or Holy Spirit (John 14:15-17), to dwell with them was fulfilled, transforming their lives and those of the thousands who had heard them inexplicably speak about God's works in their own languages. These once frightened, flawed men would from then on boldly proclaim Jesus as the Messiah and perform miracles in his Name (Acts 2:2-11; 5:12-16).

I'm sure most of you are familiar with the passage above, concerning the miraculous beginning of the church. But did you know that this miracle was not shared by everyone in the crowd? In fact, some mocked the apostles, thinking them to be drunk (Acts: 2:13). Only the faithful "devout men" (Acts 2:5-11), were able to share in this wondrous event. To the doubters, it was a message lost.

St. Peter told these scoffers that the thing they were witnessing was nothing less than the first fulfullment of the prophet Joel's words:

> *"And it shall come to pass in the last days," saith God, "I will pour out my spirit upon all flesh: and your sons and daughters shall prophesy, and your young men shall see visions and your old men shall dream dreams. And on my servants and on my handmaidens I will pour out in those days of my Spirit; and they shall prophesy."*
>
> —Joel 2:28-29, Acts 2:14-18

Two thousand years later, people are still missing out on God's message, because they refuse to believe in it.

How often does the Bible tell us how important faith is for God's messages and miracles to operate in peoples' lives? Well, Strong's Concordance lists the word "faith" some 247 times, 245 of which are in the New Testament. If the Bible mentions something that often, I expect we should pay attention. Peter continues:

> *"And I will shew wonders in the heavens and in the earth, blood, and fire, and pillars of smoke. The sun shall be turned into darkness, and the moon into blood, before the great and the terrible day of the LORD come."*
>
> —Joel 2:30-31, Acts 2:19-20

Yet all will not be lost to those perilous times, as Peter's discourse goes on:

> *"And it shall come to pass, that whosoever shall call on the name of the LORD shall be delivered: for in mount Zion and in Jerusalem shall be deliverance, as the LORD hath said, and in the remnant whom the LORD shall call."*
>
> —Joel 2:32, Acts 2:21

I now offer up a purely personal opinion as to what we might expect as the days of this age draw to a close. Jesus promised that Peter would be the rock upon which he would build his church (Matt. 16:13-19) and that nothing would overcome it. I believe that just as the Holy Spirit initiated the church in such a mighty way 2000 years ago, we will experience in our days an intensified working of the Holy Spirit in the lives of believers, just as Joel's prophecy predicted. I also believe that a majority of the church, as it exists in its many forms today, will be left out, blinded by its own agenda.

Only those who put their faith in Christ and his Word will be participants of the outpouring of the Spirit which will culminate with a grand reunion with the Lord himself (John 14:1-7; Rev. 19:7-9).

Jesus said, "Surely, I come quickly." Amen. Even so, come, Lord Jesus!

—Revelation 22:20

CONNECT THE DOTS

I'm sure you had occasion to play "Connect the Dots" when you were a kid. There on a page was a series of dots that you would connect in numerical order. At first, all you had was a bunch of unconnected dots, maybe with a few lines here and there added by the artist, but generally there'd be only a vague idea, at best, of what the finished product was to be. Only after starting to make the connections could you begin to get the picture.

Our journey through life is very much the connecting of the dots that we call "events." Now some of us may have a better idea than others of where we might be headed, but from God's perspective, our views of our respective futures remain murky, at best. St. Paul wisely stated that what we now see is but a dim image of what is really there. In my opinion, if we try to go it alone without God's help, we never will have a clue. For those who put their trust in God we have the certain assurance that one day all the dots will be connected, and we'll finally see the finished product (1 Corinthians 13:12).

But what should we do in the meantime?

1. *Pray often.* There's is nothing like talking to the Artist of All Things himself.

2. *Read the Bible.* I can't stress this enough. Why? Because the Father who created it all knows what the final picture looks like. He can use his Book to show us which dot comes next.

3. *Get others to join in.* We are all looking for answers, and there is much to be said about a collective effort, as long as the focus remains on Jesus and his Word alone.

4. *Be persistent.* This is true especially when the rough times come—and they will. Jesus said they would but guarantees he has the last word about them (John 16:33b).

So, are you ready?
Then let's get started!

PART-III

INTRIGUING

POSSIBILITIES

FOOD FOR THOUGHT

For we know in part, and we prophesy in part. But when that which is perfect is come, then that which is in part shall be done away.
— 1 Corinthians 13:9-10

CHAPTER ONE

THE VEGETARIANS
OF EDEN

I'm sure you've heard or read the opening passages of Genesis many times. In them we see that God created man and provided the garden of Eden as a place for man to live. Growing there were the fruit trees that would sustain him. Even the animals were completely tame, as evidenced in Genesis 2:19-20, when God brought them before the man for him to name. They didn't fear Adam, and they didn't fear each other, either. Nor were they apprehensive of Eve, the woman that God would create later to be Adam's companion. In this perfect place, humans didn't prey on animals, and it seems that the animals didn't prey on each other (or people). The plants in the garden provided everything that they all needed.

Interestingly enough, this vegetarian diet was retained even after Adam and Eve disobeyed God by eating the fruit from the tree of the knowledge of good and evil. After their exile, they would be fighting the weeds and the elements to grow their food (Genesis 3:17-19). Still, there is no mention of them or their offspring ever consuming any of the animals.

Centuries later, mankind had grown so evil that God told Noah to build a huge ship, gather up pairs of animals, and load enough provisions to feed them and his family (Genesis 6:11-21). Notice again, none of those critters seemed afraid of the humans or each other as they were collected for the trip through the Flood. It would not be until the waters had receded and the ark's passengers disembarked that animals would be added to the menu and develop their understandable fear of humans (Genesis 9:1-3). Perhaps, at the same time, some of those animals became predatory in their own right, just as they are today. Maybe they learned it from *us!*

Will this always be so? The Bible tells us *it will not!*

There is recorded in Isaiah a tantalizing vision of the future, when the Messiah establishes his kingdom on Earth and restores the world to an Eden-like state where the wolf shall dwell with the lamb, the leopard with the kid, the calf and lion and the fatling together—and all of them to be led by a little child. Cows and bears will feed together, and so will their young. Lions will eat straw, and even poisonous snakes will be harmless (Isaiah 11:6-9). Everything on the planet *"shall be full of the knowledge of the Lord, as the waters cover the sea"* (Isaiah 11:9b).

Once again all the animals will become vegetarians, and it wouldn't surprise me if this applies to people as well. We will have come full circle to live as Adam and Eve once did when the world was young. Yet even this idyllic existence pales in comparison to the time when God creates an entirely new heaven and a new earth and comes to live with us in the New Jerusalem (Rev. 21 and 22).

As believers, we will share in this wonderful new existence, because Jesus will have resurrected and perfected us. The Nicene Creed tells us and the Bible confirms: *"We believe in the resurrection of the dead and the life of the world to come"* (Job 19:25-27; John 5:28-29; John 11:25; 1 Cor. 15:20-23; 1 Cor. 15:51-57).

Welcome to Eternity!

CHAPTER TWO

EARLY SIGHTINGS?

Is there evidence that Jesus walked the earth long before he was even born? Let's examine this fascinating possibility. From the Old Testament we have:

> *And they heard the voice of the LORD God walking in the garden in the cool of the day: and Adam and his wife hid themselves from the presence of the LORD God amongst the trees of the garden.*
> —Genesis 3:8

> *And the LORD went his way, as soon as he had left communing with Abraham: and Abraham returned unto his place.*
> —Genesis 18:33

> *Then Nebuchadnezzar the king was astonied (amazed), and rose up in haste, and spake, and said unto his counsellors, "Did not we cast three men bound into the midst of the fire?" They answered and said unto the king, "True, O king." He answered and said, "Lo, I see four men loose, walking in the midst of the fire, and they have no hurt; and the form of the fourth is like the Son of God."*
> —Daniel 3:24-25

> *I saw in the night visions, and, behold, one like the Son of man came with the clouds of heaven, and came to the Ancient of days, and they*

brought him near before him. And there was given him dominion, and glory, and a kingdom, that all people, nations, and languages, should serve him: his dominion is an everlasting dominion, which shall not pass away, and his kingdom that which shall not be destroyed.

—Daniel 7:13-14

Verifications from the New Testament:

Then said the Jews unto him, "Thou art not yet fifty years old, and hast thou seen Abraham?" Jesus said unto them, "Verily, verily, I say unto you, Before Abraham was, I am."

—John 8:57-58

And the high priest answered and said unto him, "I adjure thee by the living God, that thou tell us whether thou be the Christ, the Son of God." Jesus saith unto him, "Thou hast said: nevertheless I say unto you, Hereafter shall ye see the Son of man sitting on the right hand of power, and coming in the clouds of heaven."

—Matthew 26:63b-64

Jesus saith unto her, "Woman, why weepest thou? whom seekest thou?" She, supposing him to be the gardener, saith unto him, "Sir, if thou have borne him hence, tell me where thou hast laid him, and I will take him away." Jesus saith unto her, "Mary." She turned herself, and saith unto him, "Rabboni;" which is to say, Master.

—John 20:15-16

And from Jesus Christ, who is the faithful witness, and the first begotten of the dead, and the prince of the kings of the earth. Unto him that loved us, and washed us from our sins in his own blood, And hath made us kings and priests unto God and his Father; to him be glory and dominion for ever and ever. Amen. Behold, he cometh with clouds; and every eye shall see him, and they also which pierced him: and all kindreds of the earth shall wail because of him. Even so, Amen. I am Alpha and Omega, the beginning and the ending, saith the Lord, which is, and which was, and which is to come, the Almighty.

—Revelation 1:5-8

Clearly we see the New Testament passages speaking of Jesus. The fact of his historical existence in the first part of the first century AD is confirmed from the independent source of Josephus who was born a few years after the crucifixion (Josephus-*Antiquities*, Book 18.3.3). Concerning the details of who Jesus really is, we have the Bible. But what of his claim of pre-existing Abraham when we know Jesus was born to Mary some 2000 years later? How can this be?

First of all, Jesus was as much a human being as he was God. Don't ask me to explain that, because I can't, any more than I can explain what gravity is. I do know that there is such a thing, because I can see its effects. Similarly, I realize that there are hard and fast rules governing the operation of the universe. According to these rules, Jesus couldn't have existed before Abraham. Yet, not only do we have *his own word* that he did but also compelling Old Testament accounts that this was indeed the case.

Jesus told us *"for with God all things are possible"* (Mark 10:27). This being so, and the fact that God is eternal (and so is Jesus), they are clearly outside the physical laws of time and space as we know them. By making this claim, it makes Jesus' "Early Appearances" entirely within the realm of possibility. Let's explore them further.

In the early Genesis passages, the Lord appeared as a *man*, not as the awe-inspiring cloud or pillar of fire of Exodus or in the radiant figure of Revelation. Instead, we see him walking in a garden where Adam and Eve were trying, in vain, to hide from his presence. Isn't it intriguing that after his resurrection Mary Magdalene is not trying to hide, but she's actually seeking him? How does she encounter him? As he is walking in a garden. But this time instead of finding condemnation as Adam and Eve did, Mary is the first witness of humanity's future redemption.

We witness another encounter, this time as one of the three men who visited Abraham, promising him a child and revealing to him what is about to happen to the evil cities of Sodom and Gomorrah. If you read all of Genesis 18 and 19, you will note that the one man who stayed behind to talk with him is directly referred to as "The Lord" (Genesis 18:17), and only two men, described as angels (Genesis 19:1), actually end up in the cities to warn Lot and his family of the destruction about to come. We are told of similar judgments to come throughout the Book of Revelation, but these will affect the *entire* world.

The first passage from Daniel tells us of a "fourth man" in the furnace where Daniel's three friends, Shadrach, Meshach, and Abednego, had been sent due to their refusal to worship a giant golden statue that the Babylonian king, Nebuchadnezzar, had erected on the plain of Dura. Instead of seeing three men consumed in the flames, Nebuchadnezzar found them walking around unscathed *and accompanied by another that looked like "the Son of God!"* The story had a happy ending for the three men who emerged totally unharmed, without even their clothes singed (Daniel 3:26-27), and the king gained a new respect for the God of Israel from that day forward. St. Paul tells us that believers in Jesus (the church) are likewise not destined for the wrath coming at the end of the age but for salvation (1 Thessalonians 5:9).

The second Daniel passage describes a vision in which someone "like the Son of man" is given everlasting dominion over the entire world by the "Ancient of Days" (no doubt God the Father himself) (Daniel 7:13-14). I've often wondered where the young prophet was when his companions were tossed into that furnace, but I imagine if he had been there with them at that time, the "son of man" he saw in his later vision would have been no stranger to him. Again, in Revelation, we see confirmation of Daniel's vision in which Jesus is to be king over the whole world (Revelation 19:11-16).

I believe the Bible is again telling us that not only is Jesus here for us today, but also *he always has been—and always will be!*

A SERMON-JESUS IN THE OLD TESTAMENT

Okay, let's start out with a question. Can anyone tell me the difference between the Old and New Testaments of the Bible? *(Get comments from congregation, and depending on the response, continue on something like this:)*

Basically, the Old Testament is B.C., and the New is A.D. In the Old we find the stories of the creation of the universe and of mankind, the fall of man in Eden, the Great Flood, Abraham's recognition that there really is only one true God, Moses epic journey with the Jews from Egypt, and more. It is the story of God's special relationship with the people he would call his own. In the New, we find the life of Jesus, the new covenant that he brought to all mankind, and the Holy Spirit's inspired writings of men given insights of faith. Now, since we've seen that the Old Testament concluded long before Jesus was actually born, I'm sure you wouldn't expect to find any mention of his life in there, right?

Would you be surprised if I told you that this is *not* the case and that there are references of the Messiah written centuries before Jesus actually walked among us? Did you know that some are so profoundly accurate that their source could not have been by anyone else except the Holy Spirit working through the men that he inspired? Well, let's explore some of them now, remembering that these were written long before the miracle in the stable or the wonder of the empty tomb.

Moses said in Deuteronomy 18:15, *"The LORD thy God will raise up unto thee a Prophet from the midst of thee, of thy brethren, like unto me; unto him ye shall hearken."* Remember, not only was Jesus the Son of God but also the Son of man as well, the young Jewish woman Mary being his mother. He was therefore a true brother to the Jews, as well as the greatest prophet and teacher who has ever lived. Prophecy fulfilled!

The prophet Micah tells us:

> *But thou, Bethlehem Ephratah, though thou be little among the thousands of Judah, yet out of thee shall he come forth unto me that is to be ruler in Israel; whose goings forth have been from of old, from everlasting.*
> —Micah 5:2

Here we are given Jesus' actual birthplace by a man who lived around the eighth century B.C.! Note how Micah says his origin is "from old." Jesus once told the Jews who were challenging him, *"Verily, verily, I say unto you, Before Abraham was, I am"* (John 8:58). In other words, he was telling him that his origin was truly "of old." We now have another prophecy fulfilled! But there's more!

Isaiah, from about the same time as Micah, tells us:

> *Therefore the Lord himself shall give you a sign; Behold, a virgin shall conceive, and bear a son, and shall call his name Immanuel.*
> —Isaiah 7:14

A couple of chapters later we read:

> *For unto us a child is born, unto us a son is given: and the government shall be upon his shoulder: and his name shall be called Wonderful, Counselor, The mighty God, The everlasting Father, The Prince of Peace. Of the increase of his government and peace there shall be no end, upon the throne of David, and upon his kingdom, to order it, and to establish it with judgment and with justice from henceforth even for ever. The zeal of the LORD of hosts will perform this.*
> —Isaiah 9:6-7

Here, not only does Isaiah speak of Jesus birth, which has already occurred by our time, but also of a time yet to come when he will govern the world forever with righteousness. Isaiah 11:1-16 gives us more detail. According to this passage, the Messiah, a descendant of Jesse, King David's father, will have the "Spirit of the Lord" resting upon him and will rule a world restored to its Eden-like state, where even the animals will no longer be wild, and the whole world will be full of the "knowledge of the Lord." In the New Testament we see Jesus referred to as the Son of David (Matt. 15:22), and that, at his baptism, John saw the Holy Spirit descending on him in the form of a dove (John 1:32-34).

Daniel relates that:

> "I saw in the night visions, and, behold, one like the Son of man came with the clouds of heaven, and came to the Ancient of days, and they brought him near before him. And there was given him dominion, and glory, and a kingdom, that all people, nations, and languages, should serve him: his dominion is an everlasting dominion, which shall not pass away, and his kingdom that which shall not be destroyed."
> —Daniel 7:13-14

The "Ancient of Days" referred to here is God the Father, and we see the Son of man (who other than Jesus?) being presented to him, after which he received the rulership of the world. To clarify a point: It is not at all incorrect to refer to God the Father and his Son Jesus and the Holy Spirit by the term, "ancient of days," since they are really aspects of the One God and share this eternal nature. And I think that's about as much as I can tell you about how the Trinity works, because an expert on this particular subject I am not.

Now then, I suppose some of you might be saying, "Well, this is pretty interesting, but it still could apply to someone else. Maybe some other person will be born in Bethlehem in the future who will fulfill these prophecies. After all, we really only see some of the things you mentioned applying to Jesus. We don't see Jesus running a righteous world government today, so maybe some day someone else will come to do the job. After all, Jesus was already here, so why didn't he establish his government 2000 years ago?

Good questions. Let me give you some more examples of why I believe that Jesus is exactly who he says he is and is the fulfillment of the things written about this future king so long ago.

Up to now, we've seen the messiah as a victorious sort of person who comes and shakes things up, fixes all the stuff that's wrong in the world—definitely a job requiring divine abilities. But there is an aspect of him which we have yet to cover. Let's explore Isaiah 52:14-15; 53:1-12:

As many were astonied (amazed) at thee; his visage was so marred more than any man, and his form more than the sons of men: So shall he sprinkle many nations; the kings shall shut their mouths at him: for that which had not been told them shall they see; and that which they had not heard shall they consider.

—Isaiah 52:14-15

Who hath believed our report? and to whom is the arm of the LORD revealed? For he shall grow up before him as a tender plant, and as a root out of a dry ground: he hath no form nor comeliness; and when we shall see him, there is no beauty that we should desire him. He is despised and rejected of men; a man of sorrows, and acquainted with grief: and we hid as it were our faces from him; he was despised, and we esteemed him not.

Surely he hath borne our griefs, and carried our sorrows: yet we did esteem him stricken, smitten of God, and afflicted. But he was wounded for our transgressions, he was bruised for our iniquities: the chastisement of our peace was upon him; and with his stripes we are healed. All we like sheep have gone astray; we have turned every one to his own way; and the LORD hath laid on him the iniquity of us all. He was oppressed, and he was afflicted, yet he opened not his mouth: he is brought as a lamb to the slaughter, and as a sheep before her shearers is dumb, so he openeth not his mouth. He was taken from prison and from judgment: and who shall declare his generation? for he was cut off out of the land of the living: for the transgression of my people was he stricken. And he made his grave with the wicked, and with the rich in his death; because he had done no violence, neither was any deceit in his mouth.

Yet it pleased the LORD to bruise him; he hath put him to grief: when thou shalt make his soul an offering for sin, he shall see his seed, he shall prolong his days, and the pleasure of the LORD shall prosper in his hand. He shall see of the travail of his soul, and shall be satisfied: by his knowledge shall my righteous servant justify many; for he shall bear their iniquities.

Therefore will I divide him a portion with the great, and he shall divide the spoil with the strong; because he hath poured out his soul unto death: and he was numbered with the transgressors; and he bare the sin of many, and made intercession for the transgressors.

—Isaiah 53:1-12

We also have this haunting account from the Psalms:

For dogs have compassed me: the assembly of the wicked have inclosed me; they pierced my hands and feet. I tell all my bones: they look and stare upon me. They parted my garments among them, and cast lots upon my vesture.

—Psalm 22:16-18

Sound familiar? If you are like me, the first time I read these passages, I was amazed. Here we have an entirely different view of the messiah—a man of sorrows who was rejected, whipped, pierced, and by his death made an offering for the sins of us all. While he died, those that killed him cast lots for his coat (John 19:23-24). He was condemned as a criminal and buried in a rich man's tomb. But even in this bleak passage of Scripture, we see that the story does not end here—God will cause him to be victorious in the end. How could this be for a dead man? The only way this makes sense is if the man Isaiah was speaking about *didn't stay dead!* Can you think of anyone else in the world who so perfectly fits this scenario other than Jesus Christ himself? It makes clear that the messiah must suffer, die, and be resurrected in order to save us all, both Jews and non-Jews. You see we are all supposed to be part of God's grand plan for the human race, and this was the only way it could be done. It required the ultimate sacrifice: Jesus' own life to make us right with God once more after our fall.

So, then, what does this tell us about the relevance of the Bible today? To me, it convinces me of the accuracy of God's Holy Word and that it is a treasure of immeasurable value. It is also a source of great hope for me personally, because as we have seen, if it was correct about the events it predicted in the past, it is likewise correct about the events yet to come.

As believers, we will have difficult times—the road to heaven is narrow (Matthew 7:13-14), not to mention rocky, twisty, and with plenty of exit signs set up by the devil and his road crew. These roadside attractions look great until we make the mistake of heading toward them to get a closer look. Yet, even when we do get off at those wrong turns, just remember that we can ask Jesus to help us get back onto the road that is the only way back home.

Trust me, it's better than the Global Positioning System, and I speak from experience.

Now I have just shown you a few things that I've encountered in my own travels through God's Word. You don't have to be a scholar or theologian to just pick up that Bible and let the Holy Spirit use it to speak to you. I mean, let's face it, do I look like the scholarly type to you?

I recommend you start with the Gospel of John, then the Gospel of Luke, and continue with the Book of Acts (which Luke also wrote). Then read the rest of the Gospels and the Epistles. Finally try Revelation. But before you do, read the Book of Daniel, because it will greatly help you in beginning to understand John's amazing vision of the future.

There are also very good chronological Bibles out there, in which you will read the entirety of Scripture in a year, if you choose this method. Get into the habit of reading it daily, even if it's only for ten minutes. Soon, your day just won't be complete without it.

Don't leave out the rich books of the Old Testament either, because that's where it all began. Try to find a good Bible Study in which you can explore God's Word with others. There is much to be said of a collaborative effort.

Why not start your Bible journey this Sunday after you get home? You'll be glad you did. After all, God wrote this book—just for you!

PART-IV

ADVENT & CHRISTMAS GREETINGS

And the angel said unto them, Fear not: for, behold, I bring you good tidings of great joy, which shall be to all people. For unto you is born this day in the city of David a Saviour, which is Christ the Lord. And this shall be a sign unto you; Ye shall find the babe wrapped in swaddling clothes, lying in a manger. And suddenly there was with the angel a multitude of the heavenly host praising God, and saying, Glory to God In the highest, and on earth peace, good will toward men.

—Luke 2:10-14

"WATCH!"

(Jesus said to his disciples) *"And what I say unto you, I say unto all: Watch."*

—Mark 13: 37

Advent is the first season of the Christian calendar, marking a time of expectation as we wait in joyful anticipation of Christmas and the arrival of Emmanuel. It is a season of preparation, of waiting once again to be wrapped up in the miracle of Jesus' birth and the miraculous tale of God himself coming into the world in the form of a tiny, helpless human infant. We are there once more, on those cold Judean hills, with the shepherds watching the awesome celestial display as the heavens are opened and the angel announces the arrival of Christ the Lord. From that moment on, nothing would ever be the same (Luke 2:8-14).

But Advent is much more than the celebration of an event 2000 years past—it is very much a time of expectation for things yet to come. Better get ready, because Jesus is coming back—and the next time it will not be as a tiny infant but as the King of kings (Revelation 19:11-16)!

Jesus says, "Watch!"

But watch for what? Read Mark, chapter 13; Matthew, chapter 24; and Luke, chapter 21 to find out. This is referred to as the Olivet Discourse and be advised, it contains some scary stuff—perhaps even more ominous because many parts of it now read like a page out of today's newspaper. This very fact leads many scholars of prophecy to believe that Jesus' return is very likely to be sooner rather than later. Though Jesus did not give his disciples a specific date, he warns, *"Take ye heed, watch and pray, for ye know not when the time will come."* He wants us to be ready for his return. It could happen before you're done reading this book. Or tomorrow. Or next week. We just don't know the time exactly, but if we are not prepared, we might miss it

Some people get really unsettled on this subject, and no doubt some would just like to forget all about it. They may be comfortable with their lives the way they are. They may be *just too busy*, so they'll put it off until *tomorrow*. Whatever the reasons might be, I doubt that it'll have much effect on God's timetable. When Jesus told us to "Watch!" he wasn't just making idle conversation. He has told us clearly that when the signs he mentioned *begin* to appear, we are to lift up our heads, because our redemption will be close at hand (Luke 21:28)!

> Jesus said: *"In my Father's house are many mansions; if it were not so, I would have told you. I go to prepare a place for you. And if I go and prepare a place for you, I will come again, and receive you unto myself; that where I am, there ye may be also."*
> —John 14:2-3

These are Jesus' promises to all true believers, and there are many more. The best way to discover them is to open up that Bible and read it.

It's all part of keeping watch as we get ready for the King's return!

CHAPTER TWO

THE GHOSTS OF CHRISTMAS PAST

Do the Christmases of yesterday hold more appeal for you than a Christmas soon to come? Do you find yourself strangely empty when it appears everyone else seems to be having such a great time? Has life delivered to you such loss and disappointment that the thought of getting through what should be a cheerful season fills you with sadness and anxiety instead of joy? Let's face it, sometimes Christmas can be tough to take.

Here are some things you can try to turn this around:

1. *Grab your Bible and read Luke, chapter 2.* Then put on your winter coat, hat, and gloves, go outside on the next clear night, and look up at all those brilliant winter stars shining in the blackness. As you do, reflect back on Luke's account of the first Christmas. When the angel, Gabriel, had told Mary she would bear God's Son, she had said, *"He hath shewed strength with his arm; he hath scattered the proud in the imagination of their hearts. He hath put down the mighty from their seats, and exalted them of low degree. He hath filled the hungry with good things; and the rich he hath sent empty away. He hath holpen (helped) his servant Israel, in remembrance of his mercy; As he spake to our fathers, to Abraham, and to his seed for ever"* (Luke 1:51-55).

Mary saw in her yet-to-be-born Son, the fulfillment of God's promise of one day establishing his everlasting kingdom on Earth (Isaiah 11:1-9; Jer. 31:31-37; Rev. 19:11-16)—a time when there would, one day, truly be peace on Earth, with Israel playing a central role.

Consider also this night that you are looking at pretty much the same stars that those shepherds in the fields saw when suddenly the sky was filled with light, and the angel told them of the birth of the Savior. For a brief moment of time, heaven and earth met. And who knew of it? Not Caesar Augustus or Herod the Great or any of the Jewish religious leaders, but humble shepherds tending their flocks and three wise men from the east who were following the star, still on the way to offer Jesus their gifts months later. God, in his wisdom, saw fit to announce the arrival of the Messiah to common folk and foreigners, perhaps because he knew only they would be receptive to these "good tidings" at that time.

2. *Read John chapters 20 & 21.* Remember the last time you were in a garden on a warm spring day, surrounded by all manner of vivid, fragrant flowers? Imagine Mary Magdalene walking in such a place, so sorrowful over the loss of Jesus that she probably didn't even notice the beauty of God's handiwork around her. In fact, she didn't even recognize the risen Lord! But Jesus changed all that, opened her eyes, and all the pain she'd experienced was lost in the joy she found that first Easter morning. If you believe Jesus, all your sorrow will be swallowed up by the unending joy you'll feel when he calls to you by name (John 10:1-5).

3. *Read Revelation chapters 21 and 22.* This is what the Lord bought for you with his own life, telling us of a time when the earth and heavens are totally rebuilt, and God comes to live with us forever in the magnificent New Jerusalem. If you believe and accept Jesus, this is where *you* will spend eternity.

I hope you'll reflect on all these things not only during the Christmas Season but also all year long, especially when the times become difficult. Just remember that in God's sight you are *never* forgotten or alone.

MERRY CHRISTMAS!

THE CHRISTMAS LIGHTS OF SUMMER

While taking my usual walks in the brisk nights of November and December, it's fun to watch the displays of Christmas lights appear in my neighborhood. Just around Thanksgiving, they begin to show up—some small, some huge, but all bringing color and unexpected light to a season where the lengths of the dark nights greatly exceed that of the brief chilly days. As time progresses, these displays proliferate, along with the expectation of another approaching Christmas with all its promise.

Before we know it, though, the big day itself arrives and rushes by so fast that it all appears as just a blur of activity and motion. Slowly, the festive lights in the neighborhood begin to disappear, one by one. The long winter nights reassert themselves, seemingly all the darker as the last displays are finally shut off and stored away for another year. It's over, and it's hard not to feel a sense of loss over those secret Christmas wishes that remained unfulfilled.

But take heart! All the lights haven't been put away! This summer, just go outside and look up! It's as if God had spread his own wondrous Christmas lights across the sky to remind us that the miracle of Jesus' birth is something which we should celebrate all year long, not just on December 25th. God, in his infinite goodness and mercy, caused his Son to come into our history, to shine light into all the dark places of our lives and to live within us—and not just for one day but for all eternity. Jesus still comes unexpectedly into our shadowy world which needs his Light so badly, yet para-doxically tries so hard to keep it out.

But the world will never succeed, despite its best efforts to do so. As St. John tells us so eloquently in one powerful verse:

And the light shineth in darkness; and the darkness comprehended it not.

—John 1:5

You and I, as believers, have something ahead far greater and more wonderful than we can ever imagine (1 Cor. 2:9). So as you look up at the twinkling lights of those distant suns slowly circling the center of our galaxy every 250 million years, itself traveling through a universe over 13 billion years old, consider that the God who made it all had *you* in mind even before that grand cosmos out there ever existed.

CHAPTER FOUR

A PERFECT SENSE
OF TIMING

It's December 26. The hurried and rushed weeks leading up to this holiday have passed, and though another Christmas Day will soon begin to fade, the event that we commemorate at this special time never will. It was a time when God literally, physically stepped into our world. Ever since, nothing has ever been the same.

Upon reflecting back at that momentous event two thousand years ago, I can't help but contemplate the timing of events in that long ago time when the *Pax Romana*, or "Peace of Rome" pervaded the Mediterranean world. Despite all its failings and often brutal repressions, the Roman Empire also provided a freedom of movement for both people and ideas, unequaled in some ways, even in modern times.

It was into this world that Jesus was born—a place called Judea, which was the last area to remain of the country of the Jews after centuries of conflict and oppression at the hands of the Egyptians, Assyrians, Babylonians, Medo-Persians, Greeks, and finally the aforementioned Romans. The city of Jerusalem itself was always a pressure cooker, particularly in Roman times, with the resentment of its inhabitants toward their foreign occupiers sometimes breaking forth into incidents of civil unrest. Particularly volatile was the Festival of the Passover, now bittersweet as the descendants of Jacob recalled annually their deliverance from Egypt to now find themselves captives of Rome. Only the might and harsh methods of the Emperor's armies kept things from breaking forth into full-fledged rebellion. It would finally occur in AD 70 when the forces of Titus burned the Temple to the ground, fulfilling Jesus' own words of almost forty years earlier (Matthew 24:1-2; Mark 13:1-2; Luke 21:5-6). At Jewish weddings to this day, the groom breaks a wineglass during the ceremony as a remembrance of that terrible loss.

The threat of Roman reprisal was instrumental in setting the stage in which the religious leaders of the Sanhedrin decided that they must put a stop to the itinerant young rabbi and his message that so challenged their beliefs and the prevailing social order. In collaboration with the Roman governor, Pontius Pilate, they found a way. Jesus was arrested while his followers scattered in terror into the night, then was quickly tried, condemned, crucified, and buried.

Mission accomplished—so they all thought..

On that following Sunday morning, Mary Magdalene was the first to discover that God had other plans! *Jesus had risen,* and for forty days he again walked the earth, appearing to those who had followed him and finally ascending back to his Father's House. Ten days later, the Holy Spirit was given to his apostles. Some time after that, a man named Saul of Tarsus, who had formerly persecuted them, became Paul, the greatest evangelist of his time.

The very nation-state which had killed God's Son also unknowingly provided the infrastructure for his message to reach throughout the Mediterranean World in a way never achievable before as Paul and his companions ventured far and wide, sowing the seeds of a new faith that could never be uprooted. It was exactly the right time, the right circumstances, and the right place.

One day, Jesus will return to bring his justice and righteousness to this rebellious world, and though we don't know precisely when it will happen, we can rest assured that God's timing will, as always, be perfect.

All we have to do is to be ready.

PART-V

WORDS OF CAUTION

Now the serpent was more subtil than any beast of the field which the LORD God had made.

—Genesis 3:1a

THE ENEMY

I find then a law, that, when I would do good, evil is present with me.

—Romans 7:21

This passage is taken from a larger discourse that Paul wrote in his letter to the Romans (7:13-25), in which the apostle relates his own personal struggle with evil. I find it compellingly familiar in my own life, and I don't think I'm alone in this, because I imagine that ever since the Fall of mankind in Eden, this battle between good and evil has gone on—and will go on until at long last God destroys for all time the source of all the misery that has plagued the human race (Revelation 20:10-15) across the millennia.

In our present state we see a duality, sometimes comically represented as a little angel on one shoulder and a little devil on the other, whispering into our ears, vying for our attention. In reality it is a much more serious thing.

What exactly is going on? I offer some thoughts.

Ever hear about old vampire legends in which the only way the monster can come into someone's house is if he's invited in? Once done, he can come in any time he wants. Because of Adam and Eve's disobedience of God's rules, they opened the door for

89

the devil to do the same to the rest of us. It's like a genetic defect which, because both parents have it, gets passed along right on down the line.

Throughout the course of history, we have seen in different individuals the way this conflict has played out. We have from the vast multitudes—the Pope John Paul IIs, Mother Teresas, and all those who have responded to the Holy Spirit's influence, whose acts of kindness may be known only to themselves and the God whom they serve. Yet there are their opposites; those that the darkness has swallowed up—the Judas Iscariots, Hitlers, Pol Pots, and the unnamed multitudes that have made the world the unhappy place it is today.

In my opinion, no true act of kindness *is* possible without the direct influence of the Holy Spirit, because no human being can possibly withstand the power of the devil on his or her own. And even *good* people, because of the weakness of our human nature, are not immune to the daily battle against the forces of an unrelentless enemy whose sole purpose is to bring us to the place where the Bible tells us that he and his followers will ultimately be sent. How do we know the devil means business? Because in his arrogance, Satan even tried to tempt *Jesus* (Luke 4:1-13)!

Only by relying on the power of the only man against whom no temptation could ever succeed can we ultimately be saved. One day we won't have the daily battle that we each face between the Spirit of God which builds us up and the spirit of this world which tries to tear us down.

> (Jesus said) "In the world ye shall have tribulation but be of good cheer; I have overcome the world."
>
> —John 16:33b

Trusting in him and relying on his strength, so can we.

CHAPTER TWO

IF IT SOUNDS TOO GOOD TO BE TRUE...

The scene below could be from the beginning of time.

"Hey, Eve, I have a question for you."

"What?"

"Did God say you weren't supposed to eat any fruit out of the garden here?"

"No, that's not right. We can eat everything except from that one tree over there. If we do, we'll die."

"God told you that, did he? Still, it looks pretty good to me. And I'll let you in on something he didn't tell you. You won't die, you'll become wise like God! Try it, you'll like it."

"You know, it *does* look awfully good..."

We all know how the story ended up. If there are any doubts, watch the news tonight on TV or read the obituaries in the newspaper. When you do you'll see that the whole world is a victim of the big lie.

John 8:44 tells us that Satan was *"a murderer from the beginning, and abode not in the truth, because there is no truth in him."*

Genesis 3:1 also tells us that the devil *"was more subtil than any beast of the field which the LORD God had made."*

So what we have here is the ultimate conman and master thief who has already stolen paradise away from the world once and will try anything to make sure you and I don't achieve it in eternity. To make it worse, he has help in the places we least expect. St. Paul warns of the devil's helpers:

> *But what I do, that I will do, that I may cut off occasion from them which desire occasion; that wherein they glory, they may be found even as we. For such are false apostles, deceitful workers, transforming themselves into the apostles of Christ. And no marvel; for Satan himself is transformed into an angel of light. Therefore it is no great thing if his ministers also be transformed as the ministers of righteousness; whose end shall be according to their works.*
> —2 Corinthinans 11: 12-15

From some of the positions I've heard being espoused from some churches today, I can believe it. But how then can we possibly know what is true and what isn't? My suggestion: read God's Book!

The more you read his Holy Word, the more you will be able to tell truth from falsehood, fact from fiction. *"Try (test) the spirits,"* St. John wisely tells us, *"whether they are from God because many false prophets have gone out into the world"* (1 John 4:1b). In other words, gauge what you see and hear against the things that the Bible teaches. Anything that contradicts Biblical truths should be treated as suspect.

But where does one start? I recommend rather than starting at the very beginning with Genesis, start your exploration with the Gospel of John, the Gospel of Luke, and the Book of Acts. Follow, that with the remaining Gospels and Epistles. The Revelation to John is the most intriguing (and most difficult) book to understand in the New Testament.

Even the scholars who have made it a focus of their studies often have differing opinions on its interpretation. But don't let that deter or frustrate you. I have found that reading the Book of Daniel in the Old Testament first, adds considerably to the understanding of Revelation. Give it a try!

I know that God will honor your efforts to spend time in his Word.

I CAN'T HEAR YOU!

Ever try to carry on a conversation when there is a lot of noise in the background? I don't know about you, but this has always been a problem for me. It's one that seems to grow as I get older. I'm not sure if it has something to do with my hearing or my ability to focus amid distractions—something that has always been a problem for me at *any* age. I suppose today there's probably some fancy scientific name for it, but I'm willing to bet that you can concentrate a lot better in quiet surroundings, too.

We live in an increasingly noisy, busy, and distracting world. It used to be difficult enough for six days, but now we find even Sundays turning into just another day to shop, to get things done we didn't have time to do during the week, or if you have kids involved in sports, just another day of practice or games to which you must drive them. Or worse, you are expected to work in a society which has increasingly turned to the false gods of commerce and profit. (Of course, Jesus recognized that it was okay to "do good" work on the Sabbath [Mark 3:1-5], and some jobs must necessarily be done 24/7. Yet even so, we should all seek out at least some quiet time to spend with him, particularly on Sunday.) On Monday, it starts all over again. Is this how God wants us to live? Here's what he said about that:

Remember the sabbath day, to keep it holy. Six days shalt thou labour, and do all thy work. But the seventh day is the sabbath of the LORD thy God, in it thou shalt not do any work, thou, nor thy son, nor thy daughter, thy manservant, nor thy maidservant, nor thy cattle, nor thy stranger that is within thy gates. For in six days the LORD made heaven and earth, the sea, and all that in them is, and rested the seventh day: wherefore the LORD blessed the sabbath day, and hallowed it.

—Exodus 20:8-11

Now for the Jews, this was the last day of the week, beginning on sunset Friday and ending sunset Saturday. Because Jesus rose on a Sunday, this is the Lord's Day for Christians, and our calendars show it as the first day of the week. In all reverence, even God needed a day off from work. He knows we do, too.

This is not just for physical refreshment, but most importantly for spiritual recharging as well. This is the day God wants you to spend with him. You see, though the Lord has appeared in mighty and unmistakable ways, such as in the burning bush (Exodus 3:2-6), or in a pillar of cloud and fire (Exodus 14:24), I believe most often he is found in a "still small voice" (1 Kings 19:12).

How are we ever to hear it if we allow the noise of the world to drown it out?

I think it's time to reclaim our Sundays and start listening once again.

THE JOURNEY

With each passing year, the disputes and divisions within many churches show little signs of abating. From my point of view, whatever issues are in the forefront, all of them center about one thing—namely that of the authority of the Bible. Is it merely a collection of dusty old writings no longer relevant in our "enlightened" age, or is it the Word of God himself? Let's examine this topic for ourselves. First of all, what does the Bible say of itself?

> *All scripture is given by inspiration of God, and is profitable for doctrine, for reproof, for correction, for instruction in righteousness, that the man of God may be perfect, throughly (thoroughly) furnished unto all good works.*
>
> —2 Timothy 3:16-17

> *Knowing this first, that no prophecy of the scripture is of any private interpretation. For the prophecy came not in old time by the will of man: but holy men of God spake as they were moved by the Holy Ghost.*
>
> —2 Peter 1:20-21

Here we have in no uncertain terms that the Bible is much more than just a collection of ordinary writings. It is God's inspired

Word. Is this bold claim supported by the evidence? Let's take an example from everyday life.

You're about to drive cross country to an unknown destination. Let's assume it's in an older vehicle with no sophisticated navigation system. I must confess that I have an inherent dislike for stuff that adds a grand or more of fancy electronics to a car's selling price. Not to mention what it'll cost to fix the thing when one day it tells you that you've just arrived at Jupiter (the planet, *not* the town in Florida.) But let's get back to the task at hand.

We buy our paper road map, and after getting it home, we unfold it (with the realization that it will *never again* resume this original configuration). After spreading it out on the kitchen table, we carefully study our route, making a few notes about towns and other notable landmarks we'll pass by. Assuming that no new roads have been built since our map was printed, we have every expectation that we will actually arrive at the place we want to be, safe and sound. Upon successful completion of our trip, we can rightly credit ourselves for our exceptional driving and navigation skills. But to be honest, we should include praise for the map and its author who accurately documented the route before us to give us a reliable guide.

Now if the Bible's source is the Holy Spirit who is beyond the constraints of time, his Word should be able to tell us of events (landmarks, if you will) we'll experience before they happen, right? Is this actually the case?

The answer is a resounding *"Yes!"* Though the entire Bible is prophetic in the sense that it reveals God's messages to humankind, some scholars have said that one-third of it concerns events in advance of their occurrences. Scripture itself declares:

(God said) "I have declared the former things from the beginning; and they went forth out of my mouth, and I shewed them; I did them suddenly and they came to pass."
—Isaiah 48:3

For the testimony of Jesus is the spirit of prophecy.
—Revelation 19:10c

Biblical foretelling of events is always fascinating even if some aspects of prophecy are enigmatic and open to interpretation. But there are many times the meaning is crystal clear. Take the following passages:

But thou, Bethlehem Ephratah, though thou be little among the thousands of Judah, yet out of thee shall he come forth unto me that is to be ruler in Israel; whose goings forth have been from of old, from everlasting.

—Micah 5:2

Therefore the Lord himself shall give you a sign; Behold, a virgin shall conceive, and bear a son, and shall call his name Immanuel.

—Isaiah 7:14

Rejoice greatly, O daughter of Zion; shout, O daughter of Jerusalem: behold, thy King cometh unto thee: he is just, and having salvation; lowly, and riding upon an ass, and upon a colt the foal of an ass.

—Zechariah. 9:9

He is despised and rejected of men; a man of sorrows, and acquainted with grief: and we hid as it were our faces from him; he was despised, and we esteemed him not. Surely he hath borne our griefs, and carried our sorrows: yet we did esteem him stricken, smitten of God, and afflicted. But he was wounded for our transgressions, he was bruised for our iniquities: the chastisement of our peace was upon him; and with his stripes we are healed. All we like sheep have gone astray; we have turned every one to his own way; and the LORD hath laid on him the iniquity of us all. He was oppressed, and he was afflicted, yet he opened not his mouth: he is brought as a lamb to the slaughter, and as a sheep before her shearers is dumb, so he openeth not his mouth. He was taken from prison and from judgment: and who shall declare his generation? for he was cut off out of the land of the living: for the transgression of my people was he stricken. And he made his grave with the wicked, and with the rich in his death; because he had done no violence, neither was any deceit in his mouth.

—Isaiah 53:4-9

For unto us a child is born, unto us a son is given: and the government shall be upon his shoulder: and his name shall be called Wonderful, Counsellor, The mighty God, The everlasting Father, The Prince of Peace.

—Isaiah 9:6

Do you know anyone who was born in Bethlehem to a virgin (some translations render the term more generally as "young woman"), who came riding into Jerusalem one day on a donkey, who was whipped and killed for the sins of others, and buried in a rich man's tomb? Is there anyone in history who endured death and yet will one day return to rule the world in justice and peace? In the entire history of the human race there is only one individual who meets *all* these requirements: Jesus Christ! I'm sure you are not surprised at this obvious answer.

What might surprise you is that Micah and Isaiah lived during the 8th Century B.C. Zechariah lived during the 6th Century B.C.!

How could these men have known about events to come *so many centuries after their own times* unless God himself had revealed it to them? Now if this is so, and it certainly appears that this is the case, then it certainly looks like the Bible is indeed the work of the Holy Spirit.

Now let's see what *Jesus'* own position on Biblical authority was regarding the mission of the church:

Jesus answered and said unto (Judas, the brother of James), "If a man love me, he will keep my words: and my Father will love him, and we will come unto him, and make our abode with him. He that loveth me not keepeth not my sayings: and the word which ye hear is not mine, but the Father's which sent me."

—John 14:23-24

(Jesus said to his apostles) "Go ye therefore, and teach all nations, baptizing them in the name of the Father, and of the Son, and of the Holy Ghost, teaching them to observe all things whatsoever I have commanded you: and, lo, I am with you alway, even unto the end of the world. Amen."

—Matthew 28:19-20

In view of overwhelming evidence, it seems that the only valid roadmap for the church is the Bible itself. Whether or not a particular denomination decides to accept this premise will determine where it carries its members—either to the Father's Kingdom or off the road into the ditch.

Which journey do *you* want to take?

THIS'LL CHANGE
YOUR LIFE!

When I was a kid, we had an old worn-out TV set with a picture so dim you could only see it at night. As far as channel selection, it was like Henry Ford once said as his first cars rolled off the assembly line, "You can have any color you want, as long as it's black." This poor old clunker of a television gave anything you wanted as long as it was Channel 8. Actually it gave you at least two images of 8, depending how many times the signal bounced off Castle Rock a mile and a half away. But do you know what? The shows that were on were pretty good! Westerns, cop shows, adventure shows, you name it, you could find it sometime during the week.

Now we have cable, or satellite, which provides us with almost as many channels as the ocean has fish. Yet despite all of these apparent advantages, I'm not so sure we're really ahead. If you're wondering what I mean, take a good look at the kind of offerings we now get in brilliant color and stereo sound. Quantity we now have, quality…I'm not so sure.

Were I to explore this theme in its entirety, it would probably fill another book…say, there's a thought!…but for now, I'll share with you the programming which has caught my attention recently, hopefully making it generic enough so I won't get sued.

I'm talking about the steroid-enhanced ads we call infomercials. I have to tell you in all fairness that I think most of them have better production teams and writers than most regular TV shows. The range of the slickly promoted products is endless—pills, exercise equipment, diets, motivational programs, new hair where none grew before—you name it. And many come with the guarantee that whichever you choose, this stuff will change your life!

I wonder, if you buy more than one of these things, will they change your life *each time?*

Now that I've had some fun with this, let's take a deeper look at this phenomenon. People are obviously watching and buying, because if they weren't, who would have the resources or inclination to keep producing these commercials? To me, this suggests an awful lot of us are pretty dissatisfied with our lives and looking to change them. And, to be truthful, some of those products might actually work to some degree. But *life changing?*

Even some "religious" types have joined this parade, promising financial success and miracles on demand, *if* you'll just send in a generous offering to their respective ministries. Now don't get me wrong, there are sincere television evangelists out there who are just as much the victims of this hucksterism as the rest of us. Why? Because they all get painted with the same broad brush, thus diminishing the effectiveness of the message that legitimate preachers are trying to get out.

In my case, lacking the funds, talent, and, quite frankly, the perfect teeth, fancy clothes, and styled hair (how does one style that which does not exist?) to go on TV, I'll have to make my pitch in these pages. (The upside is, of course, that you don't have to look at me.) Ready? Then here it is:

Say "Yes" to Jesus. Pick up his Book and read it. Get in touch with other Bible-centered Christians at a Bible-centered church. *"Ask,"* Jesus said, *"and it shall be given you; seek, and ye shall find; knock, and it shall be opened unto you"* (Matthew 7:7). You won't find your answers all at once, and there will always be more that come up. But this is a case where the journey is every bit as important as the destination; the search every bit as important as the finding. But still, how does one tell if the answers he or she gets are correct? Only if they agree with Scripture.

So if you really want to change your life—for real and forever—you'll just have to turn the TV off and get back to the Book.

EXPERT OPINION

(Jesus prayed) "Neither pray I for these alone, but for them also which shall believe on me through their word; that they all may be one; as thou, Father, art in me, and I in thee, that they also may be one in us: that the world may believe that thou hast sent me."
—John 17:20-21

It is fairly clear, even to the most casual observer of the media news, that the church is having some big problems. Now, when I say "the church," I am not singling out a particular denomination—unfortunately I don't have to, because many are afflicted with any number of controversies. In view of how Jesus had originally intended for all his followers to be one, the fact that there are so many different denominations in the first place, is a pretty good indicator that something has gone amiss.

In the two thousand years since Jesus walked the earth, there has been unending strife and division in the church, sometimes costing people their very lives. I have never been able to comprehend how those who have called themselves "Christians" could in clear conscience persecute, even kill, other Christians just because they are members of a different denomination. My God, how are we to call other people to Christ while we inflict such atrocities on each other in direct contradiction to what he preached when he walked among us?

To be sure, I'm no expert, but I offer up a possibility as to the source of much of this conflict. Remember what happened in Eden? Remember the serpent? If not, read Genesis, chapter 3. You'll see that even then Satan was doing what he does best—making a lie sound like the truth. From that distant age, the conflict between good and evil has raged, bringing us to the kind of world we live in today. Nor has the church been immune to Satan's influence...

When it was born, it's leader was God the Father, Jesus his Son, and the Holy Spirit. The basis of the doctrine of that early church was both the Hebrew Bible, otherwise known to Christians as the Old Testament; the teachings that Jesus passed on directly to his apostles while he was on earth, and those the Holy Spirit revealed to the founders of the Christian movement after the Lord had ascended into heaven. For an all too brief time, the church was truly one. And then something began to go wrong.

We see evidence of division occurring early enough to be documented in the Book of Acts (Acts 15:1-41), and the Epistles likewise address the corruption of the truth by the introduction of false doctrine (Romans 16:17-18; 1 Timothy 4:1; 6:3-5; 2 Peter 2:1-3—just a few examples). Jesus himself had warned of this before he left (Matthew 7:15-21; 24:5,11,24).

It appears that all along the way there were "experts" who felt they had the only true insight as to how the church was to be run. Of course even as some were truly right on track, I am equally sure many were in it for their own egos and material gains.

Just like *today*.

If the church as an institution can't always be relied upon, upon whom *can* you trust? Let's try the Bible since it is the product of the Holy Spirit's inspiration. To put it simply, if you see or hear someone preaching anything contrary to what is written in Scripture, the alarm should go off in your mind. If you see a preacher living a materially luxurious life and telling you that you can achieve similar results—if *"you'll just send me an offering"* to show God that you're really faithful, change the channel, or leave the building. God *already knows* where you stand.

Want to learn more? Read Paul's letter to the Ephesians, especially concentrating on chapter 6, verses10-18. Follow this wisdom and advice, and you will soon acquire the tools to embrace the truth and reject the lie.

Particularly, arm yourself with God's Word, because *nothing* is more powerful than that.

PART-VI

THE LIMITLESS FUTURE

But as it is written, Eye hath not seen, nor ear heard, neither have entered into the heart of man, the things which God hath prepared for them that love him.

—1 Corinthians 2:9

IN THE TWINKLING OF AN EYE

How fast is the twinkling or blinking of an eye? Somewhere near 1/10 of a second, actually. That may seem pretty fast, but a lot of things still can happen in that amount of time. An Olympic medalist might find it to be the difference between a silver or gold medal. A car traveling at 60 miles per hour will travel 8.8 feet. The International Space Station will move about 1/2 a mile along its orbital path around the Earth, and the Earth itself will complete 1.8 miles on its course around the sun. A beam of light can travel 18,600 miles!

But an even more amazing event will happen in that eyeblink of time, as St. Paul relates:

Behold, I shew you a mystery; We shall not all sleep, but we shall all be changed, in a moment, in the twinkling of an eye, at the last trump: for the trumpet shall sound, and the dead shall be raised incorruptible, and we shall be changed. For this corruptible must put on incorruption, and this mortal must put on immortality.
—1 Corinthians 15:51-53

There are further details in Paul's first letter to the Thessalonians (1 Thess. 4:13-18).

If you've ever heard the word "rapture" before and wondered what it meant in theological terms, this is it. I am often amazed that this wondrous event doesn't...well...get more press! I mean, look what is happening here. Jesus is going to come back and call all of us believers to join him and live with him forever. First, those who have died will be resurrected into new and imperishable bodies, and then, those who are still alive when he returns will be likewise transformed without ever knowing death! Perhaps this subject is avoided because it sounds so far-fetched and impossible. Well, consider these points:

1. With God all things are possible (Mark 10:27).
2. There are prior rapture-like events of living people who *never* died.
   a. Enoch (Genesis 5:24)
   b. Elijah (2 Kings 2:11)

3. There are prior resurrections of people who *had* died!
   a. First and foremost, Jesus himself who returned in a glorified (changed) body (recorded in all four gospels) and ascended into heaven forty days later (Acts 1:9).
   b. Some saints were resurrected after Jesus himself was raised (Matt. 27:51-54). Since they are not mentioned beyond this point, it may be that they were also raptured, but we don't know for certain.

* Note: There were others that Jesus raised from the dead such as Jairus' daughter (Luke 8:40-42, 49-56) and Lazarus (John 11:1-44), however, indications were that they still retained mortal bodies. As a matter of fact, the chief priests plotted to kill Lazarus (John 12:10-11), because Jesus had attracted so many believers after he had restored his life.*

4. Jesus promised to come back for us personally (John 14:1-6).

There is an amazing future up ahead for all of us who believe in Jesus—and it's just a blink of an eye away!

WHERE ARE WE GOING? HOW WILL WE GET THERE?

Thomas saith unto him, "Lord, we know not whither thou goest; and how can we know the way?" Jesus saith unto him, "I am the way, the truth, and the life: no man cometh unto the Father, but by me."
—John 14: 5-6

When I speak of the "church," I use the term meaning all those people, past, present, and future, who have believed that Jesus Christ is God's only begotten Son Who was sent into the world to offer up his own life to make once and for all the atonement for sin that no one else could provide. It is those who believe that He lives still, seated at God's right hand, and acts as the mediator for us all and who will one day return to gather his church from the earth to be with him forever, as He told his disciples:

(Jesus said) "Let not your heart be troubled: ye believe in God, believe also in me. In my Father's house are many mansions. If it were not so, I would have told you. I go to prepare a place for you. And if I go and prepare a place for you, I will come again, and receive you unto myself; that where I am, there ye may be also."
—John 14:1-3

The exact time and way in which the Lord will accomplish this is a mystery. Men and women of great scholarship, talent, and faith have no doubt pondered this topic since the time Jesus spoke the words that John recorded above. But in my opinion, it *will* happen for no better reason than because Jesus said so—not figuratively, not symbolically, but *literally*—a point I have hopefully made in previous parts of this book.

I believe, just as sure as the sun rises each morning, that every believer in Christ will rise to new life with him leading the way. In the following discourse I offer up a possible scenario as to how this will occur, while fully acknowledging it is *only an opinion*.

First, let's define a few terms.

What is the "Rapture?"

The definition of the word "rapture" which most closely fits our purposes here would probably be that of the state of being transported from one place to another. Interestingly it also can mean a state of ecstasy or great joy. It is easy to imagine both occurring at the same time as all those who have waited for Christ across the ages finally have their greatest desires fulfilled.

That being said, let me make it clear that *nowhere* in Scripture is this word to be found, though it is fairly easy to see why it is not such a bad term to use to describe the event:

> *For the Lord himself shall descend from heaven with a shout, with the voice of the archangel, and with the trump of God: and the dead in Christ shall rise first. Then we which are alive and remain shall be caught up together with them in the clouds, to meet the Lord in the air and so shall we ever be with the Lord. Wherefore comfort one another with these words.*
> —1 Thessalonians 4:16-18

St. Paul eloquently tells us we will be "caught up," transported, if you will, right off the earth to join the returning Jesus in the air, along with all believers of all ages. Certainly if this doesn't qualify for ecstatic joy for all who will experience it, I don't know what does.

Now to be sure, there are many well presented yet varying opinions as to what point in history it will occur. Some believe it'll happen before the Tribulation (Pre-Trib), some in the middle of it (Mid-Trib), some at the end (post Trib). Despite these differences, I am sure all Christians can agree that:

1. Only *God* knows with certainty how things will occur.
2. All believers *will* one day be with Jesus.

What is the Tribulation?

This will be the worst time in history, spanning seven years. During this time a world ruler, worse than any that have ever existed, will come and cause more misery than any of his predecessors. Occurring at the same time will be disasters of unprecedented scope and magnitude, as God himself pours out his wrath upon a world gone mad.

With these basic concepts now defined, I now offer up my personal opinions on this fascinating subject for your consideration—and hope you will study it further on your own.

The Case for Pre-Tribulation Rapture

1. *Jesus said his coming would be unexpected* (Matt. 24:36-44), and he advises us to "Watch!" (Mark 13:28-37). This contrasts with his return at the end of the age (which concludes the tribulation). This time it will be unmistakable—seen by the whole world (Matt. 24:27). Also we know that 3 1/2 years into the tribulation, the antichrist will set up the Abomination of Desolation in the rebuilt Jewish temple and proclaim himself as God (Dan. 9:27; 11:31-37). So even if the exact start of the Tribulation is not entirely clear, we get an indication from Daniel 7:25-27 that the antichrist will prevail against the saints for 3 1/2 years, and then be destroyed. Similarly, we see a 42 month period in Revelation 13:5-7 of the beast blaspheming God and warring against the saints. Daniel 12 once again mentions a time of resurrection and judgment where the righteous are rewarded, the evil

are punished. Again we have the 3 1/2 year duration mentioned, at the end of which "the shattering of the power of the holy people comes to an end and all these things would be accomplished" (Dan. 12:7). Daniel also gives 1290 days from the time the continual burnt offering is taken away and the abomination of desolation is set up, concluding with "Blessed is he who waits and comes to the 1335 days." Again this is well within the 3 1/2 year framework. This is also the same amount of time given when we see Israel being protected in the wilderness (Rev. 12:13-17).

Now, this is not to be confused with the period of 2300 "evenings and mornings" (about 6.3 years) mentioned in Daniel 8 concerning a similar "transgression that makes desolate." This appears to refer to the actions of Antiochus IV who defiled the temple with an altar and perhaps even a statue to Zeus. He even claimed to be the personification of Zeus! It ended in 164 B.C. when the temple was restored and cleansed by the Jews—which is commemorated to this day as Hanukkah. Perhaps this was very much a prefigurement of things to come.

Jesus also refers to the "desolating sacrilege" (Mark 13:14-20), accompanied by the admonition that this time in history will be so terrible that if it wasn't shortened, even the elect would be lost. Clearly he was referring to a future event, since the defiling of the temple by Antiochus had already taken place almost 200 years earlier. Therefore, to make a long story short, Jesus' return for the church appears to come totally unexpectedly, while his return to earth to establish his kingdom will be evident throughout the world 3 1/2 years after the antichrist moves into the temple (Luke 17:24).

2. *Jesus will call the dead and living to meet him up in the air* (1 Thess. 4:13-18). This would not be necessary if the church was still on earth when he comes back to establish his kingdom here. It seems to me that he will take us away to spare us the horror of the Tribulation for the following reasons:

1 Thess. 5:9: God hasn't destined us for wrath but for salvation.

1 Thess. 1:10: Jesus saves us "from the wrath to come."

Rev. 3:10: The church at Philadelphia will be kept from the "hour of trial." Though this was an actual church in Paul's time, there are scholars that state that the seven churches in Revelation also represent churches throughout history. This particular one is said to represent a "missionary church," that is, those people actively involved in spreading the gospel without distortion, despite denomination. This is the "true church," and I believe that St. John is telling us that the people who are members of it will be saved from the trials to come in the last seven years of this age

3. *The tribulation occurs after the antichrist comes to power.* I don't believe that can happen while the church is still here (2 Thess. 2:3-8). The Holy Spirit was given to the apostles on the day of Pentecost fifty days after Passover and Jesus' crucifixion (Acts 2). Jesus had earlier told them to *"Go ye therefore, and teach all nations, baptizing them in the name of the Father, and of the Son, and of the Holy Ghost"* (Matt. 28:19). This means that the members of Christ's church have the Holy Spirit living within them, having received him at baptism. I believe it is this Spirit acting through the church which inhibits the antichrist from being revealed.

Here are passages where Jesus himself tells us who the Holy Spirit is and how He works:

"If you love me you will keep my commandments. And I will pray the Father , and he will give you another Counselor, to be with you forever, even the Spirit of truth which the world cannot receive because it neither sees him or knows him, for he dwells with you and will be in you."

—John 14:15-17

"If a man loves me he will keep my word, and my Father will love him, and we will come to him and make our home with him. He who does not love me does not keep my words, and the word which you hear is not mine but the Father who sent me. These things I have spoken to you, while I am still with you. But the Counselor, the Holy Spirit, whom the Father will send in my name, he will teach you all things and bring to your remembrance all that I have said to you."
—John 14:23b-26

Without the presence of Holy Spirit-indwelt members of the church to recognize and oppose him, the antichrist will be able to come to full authority, and Satan's power to deceive humanity will be unhindered (2 Thess. 2:3-12). As bad as the world is now, it is terrifying to think what it will then become.

4. *Jesus spoke of his Father's house of many rooms which he is preparing for his followers, and that he will "come again and take us to himself"* (John 14:1-3). Again, if we are to remain on earth until he comes to rule, why would this be necessary? The chronology here seems to suggest that first Jesus brings his resurrected and living followers who had been changed at the rapture to be with him in his Father's house. We then have the seven years of the tribulation where the antichrist rules the earth. This concludes with the Battle of Armageddon that Jesus personally ends. We see in Revelation 19:11-16, details of Jesus' return to establish his kingdom. Note that he is accompanied by "the armies of heaven clothed in white linen." I think these armies are composed of the members of the church which were taken before the tribulation (reference to true believers of the church being given white garments is in Rev. 3:1-6), the 144,000 sealed Jews and Tribulation saints, both Gentile and Jew, who were killed during the tribulation (Rev. 6:9-11; Rev. 7:3-14; Rev. 20:4-6), and perhaps even the twenty-four elders (Rev. 4:4). The antichrist and his mouthpiece, the false prophet, will be cast into the lake of fire, and Satan is imprisoned in the pit for 1000 years.

At the end of this time, Satan is released once more, tries one more time to bring allies against Jesus (Gog-Magog Campaign), but his forces are destroyed, and he is cast forever into the lake of fire where the antichrist and false prophet were already placed 1000 years earlier (Rev. 20:7-10). I believe at this time the Great White Throne Judgment occurs, and all the evil people of history are resurrected and likewise condemned to the fiery lake. Death and Hades are sent there, too (Rev. 20:11-14). Now, many prophecy scholars believe this judgment is for evil people only. In my opinion, because there is mention that only those whose names are not found in the book of life are thrown into the lake of fire (Rev. 20:15), it seems to me that there must be those present whose names *are* in that book and will therefore not be condemned. Perhaps it will be those people who were mortals during the Millennium and who did not join Satan in his final act of rebellion. Maybe at this time, they too will be changed and made immortal, just as their righteous predecessors in the manner that St. Paul describes in 1 Corinthians 15:53.

Now a new earth and new heaven is created, completely free for all time of evil. Onto this new world God himself comes in the New Jerusalem to dwell with us for all eternity (Rev 21:1-27; 22:1-5).

5. *A substantial point favoring of the church's absence during the tribulation is that the church is not mentioned at all in Rev. chapters 4-18* while the twenty-one judgments are sent upon the earth. It begs the question: Where did it go? Revelation 19 seems to provide the answer, where we see the marriage of the Lamb (Jesus) to the Bride in heaven (the Bride most likely meaning the church—Ephesians 5:24-32). Here again is reference to the Bride being clothed in fine linen, verifying the things mentioned in Item 4. Again this would tie in nicely with the members of the church being with Jesus when he comes to end the battle of Armageddon.

6. *There are historical precedents of God removing righteous people from harm's way. The two which come immediately to mind are the rescues of:*

Noah and his family from the Flood (Genesis, chapters 6-9).

Lot and his family from the destruction of Sodom and Gomorrah (Genesis, chapters 18-19).

7. There are two prominent rapture-like events from the Old Testament:
    Enoch (Gen.5:24)
    Elijah (2 Kings 2:11)

    and this most significant one of all from the New Testament:
    Jesus (Acts 1:9)

8. *In Luke 21:28 Jesus said, "And when these things begin to come to pass, then look up, and lift up your heads; for your redemption draweth nigh."* It is interesting to note that Jesus indicates that our redemption is near when the signs *begin*—not halfway through them or at their conclusion.

Now what is the purpose for the Tribulation? To me it seems not only to be a time of punishment but also God's last attempt to finally get through to people, to convince them that he is who he says he is. Many will probably be converted, but most will not. It is also a time when Israel will be converted, probably starting with the 144,000. Believing Christians of today have already accepted Christ and therefore need no further convincing. God is patient, wishing that all would find him (2 Peter 3:9), yet the Bible teaches that he won't wait forever, as demonstrated with the Flood, the destruction of those two infamously evil cities of antiquity, and finally with the tribulation that is yet to come. Some people just can't be reached, even if the evidence is right in front of them (Isa. 6:9-10).

Though there will be increasingly difficult times as we approach the end of this age, it appears there is a good chance that we will be gone for the worst of them, thank God. This is a great comfort! Considering the devil's increasing influence on world events, can you imagine how much greater his power will be when he is no longer restrained? It will literally be hell on earth.

Might I be incorrect about the timing of the Rapture? That's certainly possible, though to me the Pre-trib rapture seems to provide the best reconciliation of Scriptures that at first glance might appear contradictory. I cannot in fairness completely dismiss Mid- or Post-Trib as possible alternatives, however, simply because there is so much I *don't know!* I feel much like a little kid standing on the seashore, looking out and wondering what's in all that water out there. Much of the prophetic books of the Bible can be pretty enigmatic. Daniel, for instance, is still very much a work in progress for me. But I don't feel all that bad, because even *he* didn't understand all he was seeing. He says:

> *And I heard, but I understood not: then said I, O my Lord, what shall be the end of these things? And he said, Go thy way, Daniel: for the words are closed up and sealed till the time of the end. Many shall be purified, and made white, and tried; but the wicked shall do wickedly: and none of the wicked shall understand; but the wise shall understand.*
>
> —Daniel 12:8-10

Apparently, as the time of the events Daniel saw approaches, it'll make more sense to those who accept God, Jesus, and the truth of the Bible. Still whatever happens as we approach the end of this age, I think we can all trust that whatever God has planned for us, it'll be far, far better than anything we can ever imagine, just as St. Paul said (1 Cor. 2:9).

CHAPTER THREE

THE END OF A SEASON

(Jesus told the Pharisees and Sadducees) "O ye hypocrites, ye can discern the face of the sky; but can ye not discern the signs of the times?"

—Matthew 16: 3b

Toward the end of August in my part of the world, there are subtle signs that summer is coming to an end. One can begin to see the occasional colored leaf amidst the green foliage. Instead of being hot and sultry, there is the arrival of some clear, dry days and cool, crisp nights. All of these are portents of things to come, of changes which will become so prominent in another month that we'll know for certain that fall has arrived. Of course, having seen this progression year after year, we know what to expect and how to prepare for what's ahead.

Yes, we're all pretty good armchair meteorologists, just like the people the Lord was addressing 2000 years ago. But these weren't just any people: these guys were the religious rulers of their times. And Jesus wasn't being complimentary, in fact he was criticizing them for not recognizing that God had begun a whole new event in the world and that they just couldn't see it despite their expertise. They had access to the same writings, the same prophecies as we do in our Old Testament, and even with this knowledge they couldn't recognize that the Messiah for whom they were seeking was speaking to them at that very moment.

Today we have the advantage of hindsight. We Christians know who Jesus is. We also have the New Testament. Let's see if we can do a little better job with a few of the signs of our own times than the Pharisees and Saduccees did in theirs.

From the Hebrew Bible, our Old Testament:

Many shall run to and fro, and knowledge shall be increased. Daniel 12:4b (written circa 600 B.C.). We can now travel around the world at breathtaking speeds. The acquisition of knowledge has increased far beyond anyone's capability to keep up, and its dissemination is virtually instantaneous via the Internet and satellite communication. I am old enough to remember the wonder of the first live TV transmission from Europe, via Telstar, back in the 1960's. Today we take all this for granted.

He shall cause them that come out of Jacob to take root: Israel shall blossom and bud, and fill the face of the world with its fruit (Isaiah 27:6—written circa 740 B.C.). In 1948, against all odds, Israel was restored as a nation in its ancestral lands. It has survived wars with neighbors far more populous and powerful than itself, and continues to do so today. It has been restored from a wasteland of deserts and swamps into a fertile land once again, due to its settlers' hard work. There is no place on Earth untouched by the events centered in the Middle East. More importantly, Christ's message of hope and salvation that started in Israel has changed the whole world.

From the New Testament, the initiation of the Age of Grace and new covenant of Jesus:

Now the Spirit speaketh expressly, that in the latter times some shall depart from the faith, giving heed to seducing spirits, and doctrines of devils.

—1 Timothy 4:1

Preach the word; be instant in season, out of season; reprove, rebuke, exhort with all longsuffering and doctrine. For the time will come when they will not endure sound doctrine; but after their own lusts

shall they heap to themselves teachers, having itching ears; And they shall turn away their ears from the truth, and shall be turned unto fables.
—2 Timothy 4:2-4

But though we, or an angel from heaven, preach any other gospel unto you than that which we have preached unto you, let him be accursed. As we said before, so say I now again, If any man preach any other gospel unto you than that ye have received, let him be accursed.
—Galatians 1:8-9

All these passages were written by St. Paul, who lived until his believed execution during Nero's reign in Rome. It was an age of idolatry and immorality, of false teaching and false teachers. Today there is likewise an absolute proliferation of false gospels and messages being promulgated. This is not limited to some "far out" sects but is appearing today in mainstream churches. People are being told what they want to hear by authority figures who ought to know better. St. Paul saw this coming and warned his friend Timothy (and us today) about these things 2000 years ago, and he didn't mince words about it.

This know also, that in the last days perilous times shall come. For men shall be lovers of their own selves, covetous, boasters, proud, blasphemers, disobedient to parents, unthankful, unholy, without natural affection, trucebreakers, false accusers, incontinent, fierce, despisers of those that are good, traitors, heady, highminded, lovers of pleasures more than lovers of God; having a form of godliness, but denying the power thereof—from such turn away.
—2 Timothy 3:1-5

Now the Bible teaches us that we won't know the exact time that Jesus will return, but it does tell us to watch for certain things to happen in the days shortly before his arrival. Just as the coming of autumn provides signs of its approach, what do the passages above suggest to you about the nearness of the Lord's return?

There is no doubt in my mind that the season is about to change!

Shouldn't we be getting ready?

THE END OF THE WORLD

As permanent as those distant objects in the night sky seem, they won't always be there. Time eventually catches up with everything in our universe—including the home world we call Earth. Will it be a big asteroid? A blast from a supernova? Or perhaps the most frightening and probable, a nuclear exchange of our own making? Or will it be something else altogether?

Here is what St. Peter tells us:

But the day of the Lord will come as a thief in the night; in the which the heavens shall pass away with a great noise, and the elements shall melt with fervent heat, the earth also and the works that are therein shall be burned up.

—2 Peter 3: 10

This is eerily parallel to the scenario that astronomers have proposed concerning the fate of our own sun. When it enters its red giant phase, it will probably swell out beyond Earth's orbit! As it expands, the temperature on Earth will rise, the oceans will boil away into steam, and finally, the atmosphere itself will blow off into space. Next, the solid surface will melt and the planet will liquefy. As the expansion continues, the Earth will totally vaporize and be incorporated into the sun itself.

Now if even something small like a tornado or hurricane can produce screeching wind, imagine the sound of the entire atmosphere roaring off into space and the entire planet boiling away as it is consumed by its own sun—a "loud noise" indeed!

What about the timing of this? According to 2 Peter 3:8, *"But, beloved, be not ignorant of this one thing, that one day is with the Lord as a thousand years, and a thousand years as one day."* It might be that what has often been called the Millennial Kingdom—a time of unparalleled peace and prosperity in which Jesus himself will rule on earth that is said to last 1000 years (Revelation 20:4), may actually be much longer, since God's time scale is independent of man's. Perhaps this Kingdom will actually last *5 billion* years until this earth is destroyed by the sun and then replaced by a new heaven and new earth. This will culminate with the arrival of the New Jerusalem—a magnificent city of a size and beauty beyond anything we can imagine—God's own dwelling place! All we know for sure is that *it will happen*—and on <u>God's</u> timetable, not ours.

Interestingly enough, only 100 years ago, it was thought our sun would gradually shrink and cool as it aged, so the concept of it actually getting hotter and consuming the Earth is a relatively new one. Looks like it took the smartest scientific minds on Earth only 1900 years to figure out what Peter the fisherman already knew!

What about nuclear annihilation? There may very well be a limited exchange of nukes, but *nowhere* in the Bible, to my knowledge, does it say that mankind will totally destroy itself in this way. In fact, Jesus tells us:

> *"And ye shall hear of wars and rumours of wars: see that ye be not troubled: for all these things must come to pass, but the end is not yet. For nation shall rise against nation, and kingdom against kingdom."*
>
> —Matthew 24:6-7a

Make no mistake, however, the last years before the Lord returns will be worse than anything in history, and many will perish.

In fact, many scholars of prophecy point to a terrible war occurring at Armageddon.

Armageddon (Har Megiddo, or hill of Megiddo) is an actual place where Israel's enemies will gather and bring her to her last extremity (Revelation 16:14-16). As Jerusalem is about to fall, the prayers of its overwhelmed defenders will reach God's ears, and Jesus Christ himself will return to stop it (Revelation 19:1-21). They will at last recognize Jesus as their long-awaited Messiah (Zechariah 12:10), and he will throw the antichrist and his false prophet into hell (Revelation 19:20). Israel will be restored to the preeminent state, as promised by the Hebrew prophets, and the whole world will be healed as well (Isaiah 11:1-16). This marks the beginning of the Millennial Kingdom and Christ's rule on earth.

Ultimately, even this wonderful age will be surpassed when God creates a new heaven and new earth—and comes to earth to live with us eternally in the wondrous New Jerusalem (Revelation chapters 21 and 22).

Though it is true that the world we know will someday come to an end, what lies up ahead for all of us who trust in Jesus will be so much better and, as Isaiah says below, I doubt that we will miss it at all.

For, behold, I create new heavens and a new earth: and the former shall not be remembered, nor come into mind.
—Isaiah 65:17

CHAPTER FIVE

DEATH…AND LIFE!

For I know that my redeemer liveth, and that he shall stand at the latter day upon the earth and though after my skin worms destroy this body, yet in my flesh shall I see God, whom I shall see for myself, and mine eyes shall behold, and not another; though my reins (organs) be consumed within me.

—Job 19:25-27

Perhaps the greatest mystery of all is what happens to us when we die. As far back in history as we can go, this question has not (surprisingly) been of universal concern. The idea "Is this all there is?" seems inherently troubling. It's almost as if something inside us instinctively knows that this is just *not true!* Though many cultures over the ages have developed their own concepts of the afterlife, we Christians know someone who has actually experienced death—and came back to tell. I now offer up my personal reflections on this subject—and, please understand, they are *opinions only!*

The concept of a bodily resurrection is not limited to Christians but is also present in Jewish theology. Take Job's words above, for example. Now, we aren't sure who Job was or even when the book bearing his name was written, other than the fact it was long before the birth of Jesus. We do know from the first chapter of it that he was a righteous man, quite wealthy, too. For some inexplicable reason, Job became the center of a contest between the devil and God. A lot of people find the book troubling as they read about all the afflictions that God allowed Satan to put upon this good man. Let's face it, we often wonder why God allows the innocent to suffer today. Job asked the same question: "Why? What have I done to deserve this?" Despite never getting a definitive answer, he never lost his faith, and at the end we see God restore to Job twice as much as he had previously lost (Job 42:10-17).

Out of his misery, Job spoke the eloquent and moving words written above. Perhaps this insight, born of tribulation, gave him the strength to endure all the hardship, knowing one day he would stand beside the God he had trusted upon in all his trials. This sounds very much like a promise Jesus made to Peter and his disciples, who had given up everything to follow him, many centuries later:

"And every one that hath forsaken houses, or brethren, or sisters, or father, or mother, or wife, or children, or lands, for my name's sake, shall receive an hundredfold, and shall inherit everlasting life."
—Matthew 19:29

The prophet Isaiah also speaks of a final resurrection:

Thy dead men shall live, together with my dead body shall they arise. Awake and sing, ye that dwell in dust: for thy dew is as the dew of herbs, and the earth shall cast out the dead.
—Isaiah 26:19

In the Jewish theology, as illustrated in the Old Testament, all the spirits of the dead went to "Sheol," essentially a land of shadows. In the New Testament, we get more details about this place. Jesus refers to the story of an unnamed rich man and a poor man named Lazarus—*not* to be confused with the other Lazarus whom Jesus restored to life (John 11:1-44).

After they died, the rich man went to "hell," rendered in this case by the Greek word Hades (the equivalent of Sheol in the Old

Testament), and Lazarus went to "Abraham's Bosom." From other passages in the New Testament, it is probably correct to say that the rich man was in Gehenna, a place of torment, and the poor man in Paradise, both regions within Hades proper. Though communication was possible between the regions, crossing from one side to the other was not, due to a great chasm, or abyss, between them (Luke 16:19-31).

There is no reference at all to the inhabitants of Sheol existing in resurrected bodies, they are souls only. In fact, in Luke 23:39-43, Jesus told the repentant thief that though they would both be in Paradise *that same day*, their bodies *do not* suddenly dematerialize and disappear from the crosses at death, nor were they restored to life at that time. But are we certain that Jesus and the thief were really dead?

First, the Romans were sent out at the behest of the Jewish officials to break the legs of those on the crosses. Without going into lurid detail, please believe me when I tell you that this would accelerate the death process so the bodies could be removed before the high Sabbath. When the soldiers arrived, they found Jesus was already dead. The two criminals no doubt died soon after the soldiers had performed their gruesome task (John 19:31-34).

Secondly, we know Jesus' body was buried in Joseph of Arimathea's garden tomb (John 19:38-42), where Mary Magdalene went searching for it on the first day of the week, presumably to finish the preparations on the body which had been cut short due to the arrival of the Sabbath, when the Law forbade any work. (She was to be wonderfully surprised.)

Now, it is important for us to note that it is only *after* Jesus had died and was buried that the miracle of his bodily resurrection occurred (John 20). We are clearly told that Jesus was the first person ever to have this complete resurrection occur (Colossians 1:18).

But what of the other Lazarus of John 11 and the others that Jesus raised from the dead during his public ministry? The Bible tells us specifically that shortly after Lazarus was raised, the authorities sought to have him killed (John 12:10), because many came to believe in Jesus because of this miracle. This, therefore, strongly suggests Lazarus was still mortal and by implication, so were all the others.

Another question poses itself. Where was Jesus *between* the time he died and was resurrected? Paul gives us a fascinating take on this:

Wherefore he saith, When he (Jesus) ascended up on high, he led captivity captive, and gave gifts unto men. (Now that he ascended, what is it but that he also descended first into the lower parts of the earth? He that descended is the same also that ascended up far above all heavens, that he might fill all things.)

—Ephesians 4:8-10

This passage may seem confusing at first, but to me it indicates that Jesus descended to Hades after his death and personally led the souls of the righteous Old Testament individuals out of their captivity. This quote from Peter seems to confirm that assertion:

By which also he (Jesus) went and preached unto the spirits in prison.

—1 Peter 3:19

Please note, the great apostle does not say Jesus preached to ordinary convicts in jail, but to the "spirits in prison." It seems that the only place this could be is Hades.

I am sure that some of you are scratching your heads about now, wondering if I'm really going way off base with the statements I've made so far. But please, by all means, finish this essay before you decide. After you do, *I again urge you check out the Scriptures for yourself. Challenge what I've told you. Talk it over with others, and draw your own conclusions!*

That's how we learn and grow in the faith.

That being said, let's continue.

There is a very compelling and often overlooked event found in Matthew's Gospel after the crucifixion that seems to support the claim of Jesus descending to the captive spirits:

And, behold, the veil of the temple was rent in twain from the top to the bottom; and the earth did quake, and the rocks rent, and the graves were opened; and many bodies of the saints which slept arose, and came out of the graves after his resurrection, and went into the holy city, and appeared unto many.

—Matthew 27:51-53

Could this be evidence of the reuniting of the souls that Jesus led out of Hades with their resurrected bodies? I think it is likely. Furthermore, once Jesus ascended into heaven forty days after the resurrection, these saints now at long last had access to heaven. Remember this passage?

"Jesus saith unto him (Thomas), I am the way, the truth, and the life: no man cometh unto the Father, but by me."

—John 14:6

When Jesus Christ came back to life, *it changed everything!* Now what does this all mean to us?

I believe first of all, when we die, we, like the thief who repented, go to be with Jesus—right away. St. Paul said:

For to me to live is Christ, and to die is gain. But if I live in the flesh, this is the fruit of my labour: yet what I shall choose I wot (know) not. For I am in a strait betwixt two, having a desire to depart, and to be with Christ; which is far better.

—Philippians 1:21-23

There seems to be to me an immediacy implied here in the transition between life in this world and the next. Either a person's soul ends up with the Lord in heaven or in the place of torment still left in Hades.

Here is another example of souls waiting in heaven to be given resurrected bodies:

And when he (Jesus) had opened the fifth seal, I saw under the altar the souls of them that were slain for the word of God, and for the testimony which they held. And they cried with a loud voice, saying, "How long, O Lord, holy and true, dost thou not judge and avenge our blood on them that dwell on the earth?" And white robes were given unto every one of them; and it was said unto them, that they should

rest yet for a little season, until their fellowservants also and their brethren, that should be killed as they were, should be fulfilled.
—Revelation 6:9-11

These souls are most likely those who will be martyred during the last seven years of the present age—the Tribulation. At some future time they, too, will be resurrected—probably before Jesus returns—and will accompany him with all the saints from all ages when he comes to put an end to the great battle of Armageddon (Revelation 16:13-16; 19:11-21).

I think a reasonable conclusion at this point is that, except for the aforementioned Old Testament saints who were resurrected shortly after Jesus arose, all who believe in Christ (except those who are still alive when he returns and will be instantly "changed") will go to heaven at the death of their present bodies to be with Christ and await their own resurrections in new, unperishable bodies. St. Paul gives us some excellent insight into this in First Corinthians, chapter 15.

To summarize, he tells us:

1. Just as a mature plant is so much superior to the seed, so will our new bodies be in comparison to our present ones.
2. Our perishable bodies will be replaced by imperishable ones.
3. It'll happen in "the twinkling of an eye."

In 1 Thessalonians 4:13-18 we discover:

1. Though it will happen virtually instantaneously, the dead in Christ will undergo this process first, to be followed by those who are alive at his coming.
2. We will be reunited with Jesus himself up in the air—to be with him forever. Note, at this event, there is *no* indication that the Lord actually comes all the way to earth. A fine point, perhaps, but very significant. He *will* return to earth afterward with the "armies of heaven" when he comes to intervene in the War of Armageddon, actually touching

down this time on the Mount of Olives (Zechariah 14:4).
It seems quite possible that this army will include not only
the angels of heaven but also all the saints (believers) from
all the ages.

But what about the evil people I mentioned before, the ones
waiting in the place of torment? Well, that's where they will stay
until they too are resurrected for the Great White Throne Judgment and condemnation (Revelation 20:11-15), at the end of the
Millennium, when Satan also finally gets paid back for all the evil
he's done.

Now we have covered a great deal so far, and I hope I have
been successful in presenting with some level of clarity an admit-
tedly complex subject. This brings us to the place where I wanted
to end up—a closer look at what our new existence means to you
and me.

In addition to what Paul, John, and the Hebrew prophets have
mentioned in the passages we've considered, we can fill in the picture even more from what happened at two events, namely Jesus'
Transfiguration and his resurrection.

At the Transfiguration (Matthew 17:1-8), Peter, James, and
John accompanied Jesus to the top of a mountain (traditionally
Mount Tabor). Here they had the amazing experience of seeing
Jesus changed, becoming as radiant as the sun. As if this wasn't
enough, Moses and Elijah came and spoke with the transformed
Lord. Somehow, Peter managed to suggest that he build booths or
shelters for each of them, actually *recognizing* the two Old Testa-
ment figures. After the encounter, they hear God himself praising
Jesus, declaring him to be his Son and telling them to listen to
him.

This is one of my favorite stories of Jesus' life, and only recently
did I ask myself: How did Peter recognize Moses and Elijah? It is for
certain he never saw any artistic renderings of them. (Remember,
the Jews were extremely zealous about the Second Commandment.
No images of any kind were permitted!) This suggests to me that all
of us who die in Christ will be able to recognize each other—even
if we never met on Earth.

Next, after Jesus' resurrection, we see him capable of doing the very opposite, that is, keeping himself initially unrecognizable, first to Mary Magdalene (John 20:14-16) and then to the travelers headed to Emmaus (Luke 24:13-31). We also see him capable of appearing and disappearing at will (John 20:19-20) (Luke 24:31). So what are the implications for us?

Paul tells us: *And as we have borne the image of the earthy (earthly), we shall also bear the image of the heavenly* (1 Corinthians 15:49) and that our intellect and capacity for knowledge will dramatically increase (1 Corinthians 13:12). Added to all of this is that the sin which is so much a part of being human will be gone forever (Romans 7:13-25).

All these things being so, it is not unreasonable to conclude that we will likewise have similar abilities to the risen Jesus, since *"we also shall bear the image of the heavenly."* Now comes an intriguing possibility: What if our new abilities do not limit us to the earth?

Do our roles in the Kingdom to Come extend to the very ends of the universe? Will you and I literally be able to walk at will among the uncountable stars and planets of God's entire Creation? What a breathtaking prospect!

But I think even this pales compared to what Job told us at the beginning of this discourse: Because from our flesh we, you and I, will see God at our sides—and not another! And not as strangers, either.

What could be better than that?

PART-VII

TWO PLAYS

Initially I wasn't going to include these, because I figured that they really didn't fit in a book of short essays. But after some thought (and the fact that many times I don't do the expected thing), I said, "Hey, why not?"

The Shepherds begins as two...you guessed it...*shepherds* are collecting their flocks for the night. It is one that will prove to be unlike any other they have ever experienced. It ends as...well, you'll just have to read it for yourself.

Conversations was the first play I ever wrote. I was taking a long walk out in the woods when the idea came to write about what *might* have taken place to a group of frightened, dispirited men who had brutally and abruptly lost everything that meant anything to them.

Once I returned home, the images and the words to portray them poured from my fingers into the computer and, except for a few minor tweaks, emerged as you see it here. It was one of the most *intense* experiences I have ever had, feeling very much the presence of God uninterrupted for several hours.

Though both plays are pure conjecture as to the characters' actions, they are based on historic biblical events.

I hope you enjoy them.

THE SHEPHERDS

And there were in the same country shepherds abiding in the field, keeping watch over their flock by night.

—Luke 2:8

Cast (in order of appearance)

THE PLAYERS-AD 1

Narrator
The Shepherds
Nashon—Protagonist, 35 years old
Achim—Nashon's son, 16 years old
Asa and Boaz—Friends of Nashon and Achim

The Heavenly Visitors
Messenger Angel
The Heavenly Host

Jesus and his Earthly Family
Joseph
Mary
Jesus (Infant)

THE PLAYERS-AD 33

The Shepherds
Achim-Nashon's son, now 50 years old
Joram-Achim's son, 15 years old

The Visitor
Narrator

Scene 1—At the Sheepfold

Narrator: Two shepherds have returned to their sheepfold and are making a count of their flock. They'll spend the night within the circular structure, consisting of high walls of rock topped by thorny branches.
 At least that's the plan!

(Spotlight on the two shepherds. Backlights on and slowly fade as night comes.)
The sun has just set as Nashon and Achim gather their flock of some thirty-two sheep into the sheepfold to begin settling in for the long night.

Achim: Twenty-eight, twenty-nine, thirty, thirty-one, and.... get along now!...thirty-two. *Turning to his father, he says:* They're all here, father!

Nashon: Very good, Son. We've done well so far, only three lost this season.

Achim: Let's hope it stays that way.

Nashon builds a small fire near the sheepfold's opening where the two men will spend the night, alternating as "human gates."

Achim, after making sure the sheep have settled themselves, says: We'll certainly be needing the fire tonight. Gonna be cold.

Nashon smiles: In a few months, you'll remember this chilly night with pleasure.

138

(Backlights continue to dim as the evening progresses. Stars slowly come out. One star, much brighter than the rest is centered in the sky.)

Achim nods, looking up at the darkening sky: That's true, summer'll be here before we know it. But I don't mind.

Nashon: Come and join me.

The young man puts his staff across the gateway and settles next to his father, rubbing his hands together before the fire.

Achim: Ah! This is much better!

Nashon gets out some dried meat and a piece of bread for the two of them and says: God of Abraham, Isaac, and Jacob, we thank you for bringing us safely to the end of this day and for the food you provide us. We pray for the restoration of all things to your people Israel. Amen.

(Backlights are completely off now. Only the fire and two men are illuminated.)

Achim: Amen. *He reaches over and takes some of the food.* Do you think we'll ever see it?

Nashon: What's that?

Achim: The restoration of our country.

Nashon, shaking his head: I don't know, Son.

Achim: But you still pray for it.

Nashon: Because the prophets tell us that some day a descendant of David will come and bring back to our land the glory that was once ours...even moreso, he'll establish a kingdom that will last forever.

Achim: It'll take some doing and some mighty king to remove the yoke of Rome from our necks.

Nashon: Never doubt the power of God, Son.

Achim sighs: But we haven't been free in generations.

Nashon: We were exiles in Babylon for seventy years before God brought us back.

Achim: Then I'd say we were long overdue about now.

Nashon says sharply: Listen, Achim, our problems have always been brought about by our own disobedience and stiff-necked attitudes. One that does not look so well on you, I must say!

Achim suddenly feels ashamed, and there is a few minutes of uncomfortable silence between them Then Achim says: I'm sorry, father. You know I believe in God and in everything you've taught me about our history. It's just… well, it'll take a miracle, that's for sure.

Nashon smiles and slaps him on the shoulder: With that, I agree!

Achim says: You know, come to think of it, it was 400 years before God freed us from Egypt. So, I guess we might have to wait a little longer at that!

Nashon, looking up at the starry sky: Anytime you find yourself doubting the Almighty, just look up and remember who it was that made all of that.

Achim nodded and pointed to a particularly bright star: Including our recent visitor up there.

Nashon: Yes. He certainly made that new, bright star, too. Isn't it remarkable?

Achim: Perhaps its a sign!

Nashon: God alone knows.

Shortly thereafter, Achim takes the first watch while Nashon wraps himself up in his blanket and immediately dozes off. Achim grins as the older man begins to snore.

(Lights fade for a short time, then return.)
Many hours later, Achim walks over to his father to arouse him for his watch.

Achim, gently shaking Nashon, says: Father...father! It's midnight.

Nashon opens his eyes and stretches: So soon, Achim? Is all well?

Achim nods: All is well. It's been a nice quiet night.

Nashon gets up and rubs his arms: Then maybe it will be for me, too. Even if it is such a cold one.... Achim! Something is happening! Look at those sheep!

Both men are looking at the sheep. Without exception all thirty-two of their flock are awake, but standing dead still, and looking up at the sky toward the bright star.

Achim: They're all looking up at...the star! It's like they can't take their eyes of it! What's gotten into them?

(More light plays onto shepherds, brightness increases dramatically.)
Before the men can say another word, they are surrounded by a brilliant light...and, now shivering with fear, they realize that they have company—a glowing, majestic being has appeared above them amidst the brightness!
(Spotlight on Angel)

Messenger Angel: Fear not: for, behold, I bring you good tidings of great joy, which shall be to all people. For unto you is born this day in the city of David a Saviour, which is Christ the Lord. And this shall be a sign unto you; Ye shall find the babe wrapped in swaddling clothes, lying in a manger.

(Max lighting now.)

As the awe-struck men stand mutely and watch, the glow increases and they see from one end of the sky to another an innumerable host of heavenly beings all proclaiming the same message.

Heavenly Host: Glory to God in the highest, and on earth peace, good will toward men!

Music and heavenly celebration continue as the shepherds watch in awe. Then as suddenly as it began, it is over.
(All lights off, except the stars, including the bright one. Spots slowly come on onto the shepherds.)
Achim and Nashon just look at each other in amazement until they hear other voices approaching. The sheep are remarkably unperturbed, and they calmly lay down and resume their sleep as if nothing had happened.

Asa (gasping for breath, accompanied by Boaz): Nashon! Achim! Did you, did you see it?

Boaz (likewise panting): The sky...the .. the angels!

Nashon: Is that you, Boaz! Asa? Yes! Yes, we saw it, too! Wasn't it...fantastic!

Asa: We are on our way to go see the Messiah!

Boaz: We should all go together, don't you think?

Achim: Friends, you couldn't keep us away. Let's go!

Nashon pauses.

Achim: Something wrong, father?

Nashon: Aren't all of you forgetting something? Who will watch the sheep?

Boaz and Asa suddenly are alarmed to realize that they, too, have rushed off without considering this. Achim smiles mysteriously at all of them.

Achim: I don't think we need worry. Somehow I feel that they will be in good hands.

Asa: What, you think the *angels* will take care of them?

Nashon: Asa, my friend, after what we've seen, how can we possibly doubt what God can do?

Achim: Then let's go!

(Fade to black—all lights and stars.)

Scene 2—At the Manger

Joseph, Mary, and the baby Jesus are surrounded by the shepherds. The shepherds have been talking about all that happened to them with Joseph and Mary, who appear not to be overly surprised by it all.

Achim (softly): It...it's just as the angel said.

Nashon, to Joseph and Mary: You have a beautiful son. Thank you for letting us share this special night with you.

Joseph: We are very glad you came.

Mary: Feel free to stay with us as long as you want.

Asa: What's his name?

Boaz laughs: After all we've seen this wonderful night, that's all you can ask?

Asa, slightly perturbed: Well, why wouldn't we want to know his name? It's a good question!

Mary: It's Yeshua...Jesus.

Nashon: Meaning "God saves." And indeed he will save us all, through this child.

Achim: And not only Israel...but the whole world!

Boaz: Now, let us all give God thanks for what he has shown us tonight—and for this special child!

The shepherds gather in prayer. (Lights fade to black.)

Scene 3—At the Sheepfold, thirty years later.

Nashon has since died and Achim is almost 50 years old, his face lined and darkened from the sun. Joram, his son, is finishing the count, just as Achim did for Nashon so long ago.

(As in Scene 1, spotlight on Achim, then backlights fade and stars, except for the bright one, come out as the night falls.)

Joram: Forty-four, forty-five, forty-six. All here, father!

Achim: Very good, Son.

Achim gently eases himself to the ground, feeling the weight of his years. His son looks at him with concern.

Joram: Are you okay?

Achim, smiles and starts the fire: I'm fine. Just a little stiff, that's all. Don't you worry about me.

Joram joins him by the fire: You still love this life, don't you?

Achim nods: Out here I feel free. Out here I can forget that we are still under Rome's boot.

Joram shrugs: That's just the way things are.

Achim: I suppose so. But once, I thought…

Joram: That Israel would one day be free?

Achim sighs: My father believed it fervently. I just thought maybe I'd live to see it, even if he didn't.

Joram: The coming of the Messiah?

Achim shakes his head sadly: Ah, son, I was more sure about it thirty years ago than I am now.

Joram: Because of your dream?

144

Achim nods: Uh-huh. But I guess that's all that it ever was. Even if it did seem so real.

Joram: But are you certain that's all it was?

Achim: No one else in the villages or cities seemed to experience what I thought I saw, so how *could* it be real? Besides, I've never heard or seen anything of that little child from the manger or his parents again. And dozens of so-called "messiahs" have come and gone in Israel since then. In fact, if the rumors we've heard from the other shepherds are to be believed, another one has recently been arrested and killed by the Romans.

Joram nods: I've heard that this one actually performed real miracles.

Achim shrugs: I'm sure he did. Every one of them does, right? Never mind, son. Nothing has changed. Nothing ever will.

Suddenly a voice is heard outside the hedges.

Visitor: Hello! In the camp! May I come in?

Joram gets up and greets the stranger at the gateway with typical Middle Eastern hospitality: Hello and welcome! Join us for dinner.

Achim rises and bids their visitor to come to the fire: Yes, yes, by all means, join us. It is not fancy, sir, but there is plenty of it.

  Visitor, settles down with them by the fire and takes some of the food being offered: Thank you.

Joram: We don't usually have company out here, except other shepherds. Especially at night.

Visitor smiles: I suppose you could call me a shepherd of sorts.

Achim: Well, there's plenty of pasture out here. Enough to share.

Visitor: That's very kind, but I'm just passing through.

Achim pauses and looks at the man: Have we.... met somewhere before?

Visitor nods: We have. A long time ago. I'm...

Achim looks over and winks at his son: Don't tell me your name. Let me try to see if I can remember. I want to show that young fellow over there that his old man really isn't that old!

Visitor laughs: I understand.

Joram: We've been out here for some time now. Any news from the city?

Visitor looks toward the direction of Jerusalem, a sadness is in his eyes: More of the same, I'm afraid. Political intrigue between the Jewish authorities and Rome. More crucifixions.

Joram: There have been some curious rumors that another so-called prophet met that fate. Some people really thought he was the Messiah. At least that's what we've heard. There's been some crazy stories...about him being seen again after his death!

Achim: I suppose for a conquered people like us, its easy to find solace in these wild tales.

Visitor: But you don't believe them.

Achim shrugs: Of course not. Not any more, at least.... well, there was one time.

Visitor: Tell me about it.

Achim: Oh, it was only a dream. A youthful fantasy.

Joram: Go ahead, tell him about it, Father.

Visitor: Could it be during a time long ago that a strange bright star glowed in the sky?

Achim's eyes widen.

Visitor: And suddenly did light shine all about and an angel announced the birth of a savior?

Joram: Father! It's your dream!

Achim, excitedly: How…how could you *possibly know about that?*

Visitor smiles: Because it wasn't a dream. It was real…. I know because I was there, too.

Achim: You were? Why that's wonderful! *Then Achim pauses and looks carefully at his guest, realizing something is wrong.* But wait! Wait a minute! You're too young a man to remember that night!.

Visitor: I was young, yes, Achim. But…I do recall it all—very well!

Achim: You know my name?

Visitor: I knew you before you came to the stable with your father, Nashon. I have always known you…even before you took your first breath!

Achim gasps: But…

Visitor smiles gently, takes one of the pieces of bread that Achim and Joram had given him, and looks toward heaven: Father, we thank you for this bread which you have provided.

As the visitor hands him a piece of the bread, Achim suddenly smiles in wonder as it suddenly becomes clear to him who his guest really is.

Achim: You're…Jesus! You were the baby in the manger!

Visitor nods and returns the smile.

Achim: Then you are the Messiah! And you've returned to restore the kingdom to Israel!

Visitor nods again: One day, I surely will. But this is not yet the time. My message must first go throughout the world and throughout the ages to all people! To those who hear and accept it, they will become adopted sons of God, and I will share an everlasting Kingdom with them.

Joram grabs the visitor's hands, noticing for the first time the scars, and suddenly realizing their significance: You're the prophet the Romans killed! How can this be?

Visitor, rising: With God, all things are possible. Never forget that!

Achim and Joram are overcome with emotion and fall at Jesus' feet.

Visitor then lays his hands on their heads: My friends, when Pentecost comes in a few weeks, go into the city—and you will see the beginning.

Joram, finding his voice: Of the restoration of Israel?

Visitor: Of the restoration of the whole world. Now I must go, but rest assured, I will always be near. Peace be with you both!

(Spotlight bright on Jesus, then fading as he disappears. In the sky, the bright star momentarily flashes and then is gone.)

Achim and Joram look at each other in wonderment.

Joram: Father! Did this really happen or have we both been dreaming?

Achim, looks at the bread still in his hand that the Visitor had given him: Son, I am more awake now than I've been in thirty years.

Joram: What shall we do?

Achim: Why, take care of our sheep. As we've always done.

Joram: Are you serious?

Achim, grinning: Of course. But just make sure you remind me that we have to be back in Jerusalem this Pentecost—in case I forget. You know how my memory is sometimes.

Joram smiles back: There is absolutely nothing wrong with your memory.

Achim: Make sure you tell your mother that when we get home.

(Lights fade. Curtain falls.)

Narrator:

And when the day of Pentecost was fully come, they were all with one accord in one place. And suddenly there came a sound from heaven, as of a rushing mighty wind, and it filled all the house where they were sitting. And there appeared unto them cloven tongues like as of fire, and it sat upon each of them. And they were all filled with the Holy Ghost, and began to speak with other tongues, as the Spirit gave them utterance.

And there were dwelling at Jerusalem Jews, devout men, out of every nation under heaven. Now when this was noised abroad, the multitude came together, and were confounded, because that every man heard them speak in his own language. And they were all amazed and marvelled, saying one to another, Behold, are not all these which speak Galilaeans? And how hear we every man in our own tongue, wherein we were born? Parthians, and Medes, and Elamites, and the dwellers in Mesopotamia, and in Judaea, and Cappadocia, in Pontus, and Asia, Phrygia, and Pamphylia, in Egypt, and in the parts of Libya about Cyrene, and strangers of Rome, Jews and proselytes, Cretes and Arabians, we do hear them speak in our tongues the wonderful works of God (Acts 2:1-11).

The coming of the new Kingdom had begun!

CHAPTER TWO

CONVERSATIONS FROM A LOCKED ROOM

Then the same day at evening, being the first day of the week, when the doors were shut where the disciples were assembled for fear of the Jews, came Jesus and stood in the midst, and saith unto them, "Peace be unto you."

—John 20:19

Cast (in order of appearance):

Philip
Judas, son of James
Andrew bar-Jonah, Simon Peter's brother (former fisherman)
Simon Zelotes (Simon the Zealot)
Matthew (former tax collector)
James, son of Alphaeus
Simon bar-Jonah (Peter) (former fisherman)
Bartholomew
Thomas (Doubting Thomas)
John, son of Zebedee
James, son of Zebedee
Mary Magdalene
Jesus' voice
Narrator

A group of men are sitting together at a table in a dark room, speaking in low voices, illuminated only by the flickering light of an oil lamp. A sound from outside reaches them even up here on the second level behind the thick walls and a heavy, bolted door.

Philip: What...what was that?

Judas, son of James gets up, walks over to a covered window, draws a panel aside just enough to see, and shrugs: Hard to tell...it's darker than Sheol out there tonight...maybe it was some animal.

Andrew: Then it's...not...soldiers?

Simon Zelotes: Trust me, Andrew, if it was, they'd be making a lot more noise. I was fighting those guys for years before...well, before all this. One of the best ways we knew to hit these Romans was to just listen to them coming. Stealth is something I guess they figure they don't need.

Matthew: I suppose ruling the world breeds a certain arrogance.

James, son of Alphaeus, nods: It's worked pretty well for them so far.

Simon Zelotes (speaking in disgust): Trouble is, their biggest allies are our own people who are collaborating with them. The Romans pick our high priest, and the rest of that bunch fall in with them. Some religious leaders they are! They worship Roman power and money more than the God of Abraham! They even get the Romans to do their killing for them! We saw this all too clearly yesterday, didn't we?

An uncomfortable silence falls over the room. Finally, Simon Peter speaks with anguish.

Simon Peter: And we all stood by and let it happen. And, God forgive me, I am the worst offender of them all! For all my brave talk about standing and even dying with him, I denied him when he needed me the most. Not once, but three times! Jesus called me Simon Peter—Simon, the Rock. I am more like Simon Ammos—Simon the man of sand!

Suddenly a knock at the door brings a shiver of terror to the group. A voice from outside calls out.

Bartholomew: It's me, Bartholomew! Let me in!

Matthew goes downstairs to admit him, as the others resume the conversation.

Andrew: Don't fault yourself so, brother. We all ran away when that snake Judas Iscariot showed up with the soldiers. If you want to blame anyone, blame him!

Simon Peter, clenching his huge fists: Judas! Don't speak to me of Judas! If I find him, I will tear him apart with my own hands!

Matthew and Bartholomew ascend into the room. In response to Peter's outburst, which Bartholomew overheard, he says: Judas Iscariot? Well, you won't have to worry about him. Not any more.

Simon Peter: Why not?

Bartholomew: He's dead.

Several voices: What?

Bartholomew: He was found dead in a field outside the city.

Simon Peter: Was it the Romans? The temple guards?

Bartholomew shakes his head: No, from what I heard it was either suicide or an accident. The body was pretty badly damaged when it was found, so no one knows for sure.

Simon Peter smiles without any real joy: I hope he enjoys the fires of Gehenna. My only regret is that I didn't get to send him there myself.

Andrew: Judas will surely face the Almighty's justice for what he did. We have seen in our own Scriptures how it went for all those who opposed God.

Simon Peter: I hope God's curse falls on *all* the men who orchestrated and carried out this...this murder!

Matthew, putting his hand on Peter's shoulder: "Love your enemies, bless them that curse you, do good to them that hate you, and pray for them which despitefully use you, and persecute you."

Simon Peter: Huh?

Matthew: It was something he said…something the Lord said when we first started out. I never forgot it.

John: You're right…and there was something more, something I heard before he died.

There is a pause as John tries to collect himself.

Simon Peter: Well? What was it?

John swallows hard and says: He…he said, "Father, forgive them; for they know not what they do."

Simon Peter: Are you sure? How could this be?

John: I don't know. "Forgive them." That's what he said!

Simon Peter shakes his head: I'm afraid I just can't do it. I can't bring myself to pray for those who killed him…any more than I could admit to knowing him the other night.

For a while, the silence returns to the room. Thomas finally speaks.
Thomas: So, what do we do now?

Judas, son of James: Do now?

Thomas: It's a simple enough question. What do we do from here on out? Any of you thought about that lately?

Simon Peter looks over at him and shrugs: If I live through this, I guess I'll go back to fishing. It's all I know. What about it, Andrew? Does that sound good to you?

Andrew nods: I suppose so, Peter. What else do we have?

John: That was our trade, too. James, and mine. Our father's kept the business going. He'll welcome us back, I'm sure.

James, son of Zebedee: If we can ever get him to trust us again after walking away like we did.

John: Dad's a good man. I think he knew Jesus was special. Remember the huge catch of fish we had before we left? Besides, if Jesus could convince Simon Peter to come along...after all everyone knows that Simon Bar-Jonah is no one's fool!

Simon Peter: I appreciate the compliment, but after the past couple of days, I've been the biggest fool of all...if only I had made a stand when I had the chance!

Andrew: You would've gotten yourself killed, too.

Simon Peter: Maybe that would've been better than having to remember the look in Jesus' eyes when I denied him.

Andrew: Look, none of us are blameless. We all did the same thing. We're all guilty.

There is a murmur of assent from the others in the room.

After a few uncomfortable moments, Andrew says: But we can't change what's happened. And Thomas is right. We must think of the future. So tell me, Thomas, where will you go from here?

Thomas looks at the men and suddenly stands up: Gentlemen, I'm going home! This very moment!

Bartholomew: Are you mad? That might be exactly where the authorities expect you to show up!

Thomas: I'll take my chances. I'm just done sitting around here waiting for the end. If it comes, it comes.

Andrew: Please, be reasonable!

Thomas: Look, I'm going to say what I think most of you have been thinking. It's over! The dream died along with the Rabbi. I've been away for three years now. It's time to go.

Bartholomew begins to nod: Maybe...maybe he's right.

Thomas: Are any of you leaving with me?

Simon Peter: I do intend to go back myself, as I said. But not right now. Not tonight. I just need to be here, in this place…where he was…just for a little while longer.

The others nod in agreement.

Thomas: Then may the Lord bless and watch over all of you!

Simon Peter walks over and clasps the man's hand: Shalom! Go with God, my friend!

Thomas picks up his few possessions, turns, faces his friends once more with a sad smile, and leaves. Trying to break up the melancholy, Simon Peter turns to Matthew:

Simon Peter: And how about you, Matthew? What will you do with yourself?

Despite the oppressive atmosphere, Matthew answers with a faint smile: I guess I can't go back to the tax office again, now can I?

Simon Peter: No, I don't suppose you can at that. Especially since Simon the Zealot over there knows your face so well. And we all know his attitude on the subject of Roman collaborators.

Matthew: Perhaps your fishing business could use a good accountant.

Simon Peter (smiling): I'll see what I can do. Now then, Simon Zelotes, since your name came up, it's your turn. Would you like to come into the fishing business?

Simon Zelotes: I'm afraid I'm not very much the seaman type. Not comfortable in the water. Thanks anyway.

Andrew: Then what are your plans?

Simon Zelotes: I still have a lot of friends out in the hills. And I have even more reason to hate the Romans now!

John: How can you have been with us so long and feel that way?

Simon Zelotes: Because that's the way the world works, John, okay? If you haven't figured that out by now, especially by what's happened to our Master who did nothing but good, then you are living in a fool's paradise. My friends and I may not be able to throw the Roman legions out of our country, but, by heaven, we can make things difficult for them.

John: If they catch you, they'll crucify you!

Simon Zelotes: At least I'll have the satisfaction of knowing I got a lot of them before they got me!

Simon Peter, angrily: Haven't you seen enough bloodshed lately, Simon?...Haven't you all?

They all look at each other, ashamed of so soon forgetting what Jesus had tried to show them.

Simon Zelotes: I...I'm sorry, John, Peter. I'm sorry, all of you. It's just that after these past couple days...

John smiles and nods: Forget it, Simon. I already have. It's late. We're all tired.

Simon Peter, looking out the small section of uncovered window: You're right, John. In fact it's so late its tomorrow morning! It's the third day since...he died.

John: And we've been up all night—again! It'll be sunrise in an hour or so.

Simon Peter, suddenly getting a strange look on his face, says to John: You know, for some reason, I'm not very tired right now. And I just feel the need to get out of here for a little while, before the crowds start milling around. Anyone want to join me?

John: Sure, Peter. I'll go along. Besides I think it'll be safer if you don't go alone.

Matthew: But Peter, you just told Thomas...

Simon Peter: Never mind what I told him. I changed my mind. I need some fresh air. I'll be back, don't worry. Coming, John?

John: Right behind you.

Despite repeated protestations, they both leave the others behind.

Matthew: That's two more. Now we are only eight.

James son of Zebedee: I can see where your training in numbers will be valuable in the fish business.

Matthew (smiles): Want to hire me on, too? Your place isn't far from Simon Peter's. Maybe I can work out a discount.

James son of Zebedee (smiles back): I'll consider it after I get some sleep. Maybe that's something we should all do. We need to be rested and alert for whatever is coming next.

It wasn't long before they all succumbed to exhaustion (lights fade out). But in less than an hour, they were awakened by the sounds of pounding, and familiar voices on the door below:

Simon Peter: Open up! Quick! Let us in!

(Lights come up quickly as Simon Zelotes lets them in, chiding them for the commotion.)

Simon Zelotes: Why not just sound the trumpets, you two? Let the Romans and the Sanhedrin know exactly where we are.

Gasping for breath, John says: We've been to the tomb where Jesus was. Something just drew us there, both of us....He's gone!

Simon Zelotes: What are you saying?

John: The Lord is gone, I tell you! The stone was rolled away, and the tomb was empty except for the grave cloths!

Simon Zelotes: Those Roman swine! As if killing him wasn't enough! Now they've stolen the body!

Simon Peter: I don't think it was them. That tomb had been completely secured—with Roman guards. We met Mary Magdalene out there, and that's what she said. But that wasn't all. She was quite beside herself and told us an incredible story! So we went to see for ourselves, and it was just as she had said!

Simon Zelotes: It was the Romans, I tell you! They stripped his body before stealing it. They dishonor us even in death!

Simon Peter, shaking his head: The shroud was just lying there, the face cloth rolled up in another place by itself—all undamaged. Why would the Romans, or any other grave robbers, do that? Besides, there were no valuables put in there to steal. It may have been a wealthy man's tomb, but it was common knowledge that Joseph of Arimathea had let Jesus be buried there. None of this makes any sense at all! But that wasn't the end of her tale. She also said...

At this moment, another rap comes from the door, followed by a woman's voice.

Mary: Simon! John! It's Mary!

Simon heads for the door and says: She can tell you herself what she told us!

Immediately he leads her upstairs. She is still catching her breath, but strangely radiant and smiling.

Mary: How much have you told them?

John: Up to where we saw the tomb. Why don't you finish?

Mary nods: I saw angels at the tomb! And then I saw Jesus himself. I didn't even recognize him at first, but He spoke to me! He has risen from death! The Lord is alive!

The disciples looked at each other, all genuinely concerned for her. Simon Peter guides her with his big, rough hands to the table: There, now, Mary, I know it was awful what's happened these past few days, and now finding Jesus' tomb broken into. It's been a terrible shock!

158

Looking at him with clear, lucid eyes, Mary smiles a brilliant smile: Peter, I am not mad, nor hysterical. Jesus is alive, and he's given me a message...for all of you! That's why I'm here.

Simon Peter, unable to take his eyes from hers: All right. What did he want you to tell us?

Mary: That he would soon come to see you. I suggest you stay here and wait. It'll be safer. The authorities are still prowling around. They haven't forgotten about you, you know.

Matthew: Peter, she's probably right—about us staying put a little while longer, at least.

Mary, still beaming: Listen, I know it sounds crazy, I really do. But I think you'll soon see I've told the truth. Now I must be getting home.

Simon Peter: You're welcome to stay here with us. Maybe you'll... uh...see him when he arrives.

Mary, getting ready to leave: Ah, Simon, but I've seen him already.

Simon Peter: As you wish, Mary. Thank you for coming. Please take care of yourself. Come and get us if you need anything.

Mary: You will see him for yourselves. Very soon!

Mary leaves, and they all shake their heads sadly for her.

John: I hope she'll be all right.

Simon Zelotes: I wonder now if madness is to be our fate on top of being wanted men?

(Lights fade as evening comes. Suddenly the room is filled with one brilliant light.)

The disciples look toward the light, facing the audience. The audience hears Jesus voice.

Jesus: Peace be with you!

All the men fall to their knees, Simon Peter speaks: My Lord! Is it...is it really you?

Jesus: Yes, my friends. Peace be with you all.

John: Lord, you really are alive!

Jesus: Yes, John. And I will live forever. And because this is true, you will also. Now then, there is much we have to talk about and much you all have to accomplish. As the Father has sent me, so now I send you!

(Light fades to black.)

Narrator: For the next forty days, Jesus appeared and taught his disciples. We don't know everything he did, but we know it was extensive. According to the Gospel of John we read:

> *"And there are also many other things which Jesus did, the which, if they should be written every one, I suppose that even the world itself could not contain the books that should be written."*
> —John 21:25

After this, Jesus rose into heaven, and ten days later, on the day of Pentecost, the disciples received the Holy Spirit, and the church was born.

Oh yes, one more thing: Remember Thomas who had left? He didn't get to see Jesus when he first appeared, and he didn't believe what his friends told him any more than they originally believed Mary Magdalene. But a week later, when Thomas was with them all again, he saw Jesus for himself.

So let us never forget that *"neither death, nor life, nor angels, nor principalities, nor powers, nor things present, nor things to come, nor height, nor depth, nor any other creature, shall be able to separate us from the love of God, which is in Christ Jesus our Lord"* (Romans 8:38-39).

And that includes locked rooms, too!

EPILOGUE

We've come to the parting of the ways, and though this particular journey has come to an end, the study of God's Word never will. For thousands of years people just like us have read its inspired pages, told and retold its wonderful stories.

From the vastness of time and space and for reasons known to God alone, he has caused us to *be*, to look up and to wonder. He has created human beings—marvelous paradoxes—capable of sublime acts of nobility when connected to the Creator and depraved acts of evil when left on their own. From the sons and daughters of Adam and Eve came God in human form, as Jesus Christ, and from them also will come the antichrist in the last dark days of this age on earth.

All throughout history God has given individuals the ability to choose which way they have wanted to go—along with the subsequent rewards or consequences depending on the paths chosen. Either we can "go it alone" or "go it with God."

In the end, it's all up to us.

I hope this book will in some small way help you to make the *right* decision!

APPENDIX

A QUICK OVERVIEW OF THE BIBLE

The Old Testament

I. *LAW.* The Pentateuch (the five books of Moses or the Torah). <u>Genesis to Deuteronomy.</u>
    A. Genesis is a history of the Creation all the way up to the story of Jacob's family seeking refuge in Egypt under Joseph during a great famine.
    B. Exodus through Deuteronomy concern the Jews' flight from Egypt, wanderings through the desert, the giving of the law, and their arrival at the Promised Land.

II. *HISTORY.* <u>Joshua through Esther.</u> More Jewish history of life in their new land and what happened to them there.
III. *POETRY AND WISDOM: THE WRITINGS.* <u>Job through the Song of Solomon.</u> Here we have inspired writings of Job's trials and enduring faith, King David, King Solomon, and many others.
IV. THE PROPHETS
    A. Major Prophets-<u>Isaiah through Daniel</u>
    B. Minor Prophets-<u>Hosea through Malachi</u>

The terms "major prophets" and "minor prophets" are not to be seen as characterizations of the importance of their various messages from God to the people, but reflect only on the lengths of their respective books. They were not solely prognosticators, either, but God's messengers to the people of Israel to try to get them back on track to God's wishes and the consequences of not doing so. Some of their declarations, though, did include tantalizing glimpses of the events of future times, including the restoration of Israel (Isaiah 4:2-6, 25:6-8; Jeremiah 23:7-8) and the coming of the Messiah (Isaiah 11:1-16, 52:13-15, 53:1-12; Jeremiah 23:5-6; Daniel 7:13-14 to name a few). I hope you'll look these up yourself, by the way. When you do, just remember that these passages were written *many centuries* before the birth of Jesus. These astoundingly accurate descriptions of future events seem to have only one possible source—that of the Holy Spirit who is unfettered by constraints of time and space. Indeed, it is my belief that God truly is the source of the *entire* Bible.

THE NEW TESTAMENT

I. *LAW.* The Gospels—the Good News. <u>Matthew through John.</u> All four chronicle the life of Jesus and show us the New Covenant.

II. HISTORY. <u>The Acts of the Apostles.</u> An account written by Luke of the beginning of the Christian Church.

III. *THE WRITINGS.*

    A. St. Paul's letters of exhortation and instruction to the early churches containing profound wisdom and insight. <u>Romans through Philemon.</u>

    B. Letters written by others providing guidance to the early church, still, just like Paul's letters, applicable to us today. <u>Hebrews through Jude.</u>

IV. *PROPHECY.* <u>The Revelation to John (the Apocalypse)</u>, also written by the man whose gospel bears his name, while exiled on the island of Patmos for standing firm in the faith. It is a book full of symbolism, perhaps the most difficult one to interpret. It does convey both disturbing images of the fate awaiting unbelievers and an enthralling vision of the paradise God has planned for those who have accepted Jesus. Particularly moving is the description of the culmination of history, when God himself will come to live with us again (in chapters 21 and 22). Want a lift in your spirit? Read those two chapters.

The Gospels incorporate history and Jesus' New Covenant, or new law, if you wish. Acts is a recollection of early church history. The Epistles reflect the wisdom of the early founders and leaders of the church, and finally, Revelation is a prophetic document, rich in symbolism, which assures us that one day all believers will live forever—a joyful eternity in God's presence.

We see in the Bible the whole story—the creation of the universe, the paradise of Eden, our expulsion, Jesus' atoning sacrifice of his own life to make us right with God once more, the final battle between God and Satan (in which the devil is finally and forever condemned along with all of his minions), and the recreation of the world and the heavens where God will live among us forever in the New Jerusalem.

BIBLIOGRAPHY

Good News Bible, American Bible Society, New York, New York, U.S.A., 1976

Holy Bible—King James Version, World Bible Publishers, Iowa Falls, Iowa, U.S.A.

Holy Bible—New Living Translation, Tyndale House Publishers, Inc., Wheaton, Illinois, 1996

Holy Bible—Revised Standard Version, Thomas Nelson and Sons, New York, U.S.A.; Toronto, Canada; London, England, 1952

Kerr, William F., *Kregel Bible Handbook,* Originally published: *Kerr's Handbook to the Bible,* Kregel Publications (a division of Kregel Inc.), P.O. Box 2607, Grand Rapids, MI, 49501, 2000

McGeveran, William A. Jr. (Editorial Director), *The World Almanac and Book of Facts,* World Almanac Books (a division of World Almanac Education Group, Inc.), 512 Seventh Avenue, New York, New York, 10018

One Year Chronological Bible—New International Version, Tyndale House Publishers, Inc., Wheaton, Illinois, 1995

Strong, James, L.L.D., S.T.D., *The New Strong's Exhaustive Expanded Concordance of the Bible, Red Letter Edition.* Thomas Nelson Publishers, Nashville, Tennessee, U.S.A., 2001

Vigorito, Catherine Galasso, *A New You,* Adams Media Corporation, Avon, Massachusettes, U.S.A., 2003

Whiston, William (translator), Paul Maier (commentator), *The New Complete Works of Josephus,* Kregel Publications (a division of Kregel Inc.), Grand Rapids, MI, 49501, 1999

Wyatt, Stanley P., *Principles of Astronomy,* Allyn and Bacon, Inc., 470 Atlantic Ave., Boston, Mass., 1971,

Printed in the United States
76251LV00006B/46-60